Single, Married, Separated, and Life After Divorce

by
Myles Munroe

Destiny Image® **Publishers, Inc.**
P.O. Box 310
Shippensburg, PA 17257-0310

"Speaking to the Purposes of God for This Generation
and for the Generations to Come"

Bahamas Faith Ministry
P.O. Box N9583
Nassau, Bahamas

ISBN 1-56043-094-X

For Worldwide Distribution
Printed in the U.S.A.

Twenty-third Printing: 2000   Twenty-fourth Printing: 2000

More than 125,000 in print

This book and all other Destiny Image, Revival Press, MercyPlace, Fresh Bread, and Treasure House books are available at Christian bookstores and distributors worldwide.

For a U.S. bookstore nearest you, call **1-800-722-6774**.
For more information on foreign distributors,
call **717-532-3040**.
Or reach us on the Internet: **http://www.reapernet.com**

Contents

Foreword by Oral Roberts   5

Introduction   7

1 The Myth of Singleness   9

2 God Wants You To Be Single   17

3 The Advantage of Being Unmarried   25

4 An Omelet Is Only as Good
as the Eggs   29

5 Singleness Is God's Joy   35

6 Prepared for Marriage   39

7 We Live in Two Worlds   43

8 Remain in the Station
Where God Called You   51

9 Divorce and the Bible   55

10 The History of Divorce   65

11 The Husband's Responsibility   75

12 Broken Relationships   85

13 The Traumas of Divorce   93

14 The Aftermath of Trauma   101

15 Emotional Aftershocks   111

16 Life After Divorce
and Separation   119

Dedication

I warmly dedicate this book to the most wonderful woman I have ever met, my precious, darling wife, Ruth, and to the future that God is allowing us to be stewards of.

...to my two dear children, Charisa and Chairo (Myles, Jr.).

...to the many prayerful members and supporters of Bahamas Faith Ministries International Fellowship.

...to the third world people in every nation.

I would further like to thank a number of special people who have contributed to my life and to the success of this project. Thank you to Mr. George Vinnett and his able and efficient staff for their help in transcription, production and development of this project. I believe the commitment of Vincom to the integrity of the Word of God and quality publications is a testimony to the new breed of leadership rising in the Church today.

Foreword

I am excited about Myles Munroe, his ministry that's always on the cutting edge, and this most unusual book. If you read it as carefully as I did the manuscript, you simply won't put it down. It will provoke you, make you look at the scriptures again, and pay more attention than you ever have to the real myth of singleness.

Divorce or remarriage or both will take on a new meaning in the light of Who wrote the book about it: God and His Son, Jesus Christ. You will learn something about your singleness if you are not married, or your singleness if married, without which you probably will never be happy and fulfilled, as God intended.

Myles, seven years as a student at Oral Roberts University in the seventies, from the Bahama Islands, meant business with God, with himself, with all of us. By the sheer force of his spirit and mind, he stood out. In the clipped British accent, under which he was reared, we could understand precisely what he was saying. When he called me by my official title at ORU, ''President Roberts,'' it was not only with perfect diction but with respect. When we're together today, he speaks the same way. Because he was far from home, he thought of Evelyn like he did his gracious mother. He called her, ''Mama,'' and endeared himself to her forever.

I make these personal references to indicate, you will find he writes as clearly as he speaks and as succinctly, getting both into your spirit and mind, leaving you with an impact that will touch you to the core of your being.

I am proud of Myles and of this book and am grateful it's now available to the Body of Christ...and to those who will enter the Body when they read it.

Oral Roberts

Introduction

There are few human experiences that are more tragic, devastating, and generationally impacting than divorce. Perhaps you will agree that few of us can say we have not been touched, affected, or do not know someone who has been hit by this traumatic social spectre.

I have traveled to many countries with varied cultural differences and unique social settings. And I have spoken and lectured in seminars, conferences, and conventions across the complete spectrum of socio-economic strata. I have seen the scars of divorce manifest themselves like open wounds oozing with hurt, bitterness, hatred, and disillusionment.

You may be amazed to learn that in many of my audiences, up to 60 percent either have been divorced or are products of a divorce situation.

Much of modern society around the world is experiencing the negative results of this relationship tragedy. In simple terms, divorce is the physical and legal termination of a marital vow that was intended to last forever.

In counseling thousands of individuals, I must conclude that I have not seen any experience more traumatic than a divorce. The emotional effect is unbearable, the physical toll is astounding, the spiritual impact is immobilizing, and the social cost can be self-inflicted isolation and low self-esteem.

This business of divorce is a very complex issue. Divorce seems to create more problems than it solves. Years later, many still grapple with the spiritual, moral, and religious elements related to divorce. Then there are the legal, social, economic, and material (settlements and/or restricted finances on both sides) aspects of divorce.

Most tragic of all is the toll on children and on the institution of the family. The "ripple effect" of such an experience is astonishing in its impact on people even after the event is legally concluded.

But, have you ever noticed that divorce is impossible without marriage? Marriage must precede divorce and is a requirement *for* divorce. Considering this fact, it ought to be obvious that marriage is *more* important than divorce. Perhaps this is the key to making divorce impossible.

Therefore, any exploration of the issue of divorce and its causes is important to everyone — single, married, separated, or divorced.

As a matter of fact, the effects of divorce are the same for anyone who has ever experienced a break in — or the termination of — a well-bonded, emotional relationship with another individual. This includes those who are married but separated, those who have been "jilted" or abandoned by a lover, those who go through the death of a loved one, or those who have experienced the separation of close friends.

The trauma, loneliness, sense of loss, effects on self-esteem, and battles or struggles with bitterness, hatred, and jealousy are the same for everyone who experiences "divorce."

In this book, we will take a close look at the criticalness of being a "single, separate, unique, and whole" person in Christ before marriage, the importance of being joined together in Christ in marriage, and the very serious issues of separation and divorce. We will look at what the Bible has to say about these areas. Then, what about remarriage? What do you do with the hurt? How do you forgive? Let us begin.

"It's okay to be single,
but not good to be alone."

1

The Myth of Singleness

My secretary buzzed to say my next appointment had arrived. I walked to the door to meet and welcome the person who, up to that moment, had been only a name in my appointment book.

A beautiful young lady dressed neatly and smartly walked in and sat down.

She suddenly blurted out, "I can't take it anymore. I am tired of being single. I need a mate *now*. I am growing older, and life is passing me by. What's wrong with me? Why does no man want me? I must be ugly. There must be something wrong with me. I feel like killing myself. *Please* help me!"

Those words were not strange to me — I had heard them many times. Over the years I have had to help thousands of individuals find their balance and review their concepts of life. So I shared with her the "myth of singleness."

There is a "myth" or an erroneous conception of singleness. As a matter of fact, people do not have a "singleness problem." They have an entirely different problem called "being single."

Some of the things in this book may shock you, but please keep reading until you explore the entire content of this book.

First, let us consider the concept of that ever-abiding concern which seems to control and influence so many lives — ''singleness.''

What *is* ''singleness''?

What does it mean to be single?

Any dictionary definition will have these words, or synonyms for them: ''to be separate, unique, and whole.''

Would you like to stop being whole or a unique person? Would you like to lose your identity? Of course not. So what is the problem with singleness?

There is no problem. The problem is with our definition, which has been given to us by a cultural, socio-economic system under the rulership of Satan, the god of this ''world order.'' (2 Cor. 4:4.) The world's definition, which the Church has adopted, opens the door to hurt, rejection, and even self-hatred.

We have confused *singleness* with ''being alone.''

Will there ever be a time, and has there ever been a time, when you will cease to be ''separate, unique, and whole''?

Should there ever be a time when you cease to be a single being who is unique and whole?

If your answer is ''no,'' then the next question is:

Does getting married do away with this definition of being single?

When you marry, do you stop being a single individual who is unique and whole?

Furthermore, the Bible does not teach that singleness is bad, negative, or unhealthy.

If *a state of singleness* means "to be unique and whole," then to be totally single should be every Christian's number one goal. In fact, I want to impress upon you in this book that no one should marry until he or she is totally single. Until you are a separate, single, unique, and whole person, you actually are not ready to marry!

Marriage counselors, whether Christian or secular, will tell you that 99 percent of marital problems arise because a husband or wife (or both) have not seen themselves as unique, worthy individuals; i.e., they have a bad self-image, or they are schizophrenic in some way and not whole, or they are not separate but always depend on some other person to make them happy. What I am saying is that *until you are truly single*, marriage will be a difficult, and perhaps negative, experience.

Your marriage will get better as you become *more* single.

I am striving to be truly single, and I believe that, instead of running *from* being single, you should be running *toward* singleness. However, let us do as every wise person should do about every subject and see what the Author and Creator of the product has to say about this subject.

God's View of Singleness

In Genesis 2:18, did God say, "It is not good for man to be single"?

No, He said, ". . . **It is not good that the man should be** *alone***. . . ."**

God had no problem with the man's separateness, his uniqueness, or his wholeness. As a matter of fact, Adam did not *know* that he was alone. God's statement was predicated on His own observation of the situation, on His own wisdom.

The implication is that Adam was so totally unique and so whole that he did not miss anybody. He was so "together," so separate, and so complete in himself that he did not even know he needed anyone else. Having a companion was not Adam's idea, but God's.

Another thing that you need to see is that *Adam did not need a wife*. That is another misconception we have gotten from traditional thinking.

God did not say, "Adam is not a whole being, so I will make him a wife to complete him."

In essence, God said, "I am going to make him a helper who will be compatible, or suitable, or like him; another being who will complement him and be complemented by him."

The "marriage" came a few verses down. We put the marriage in verse 18 when it is not there. Verse 18 simply tells us of God creating a second human being. In verse 22, Moses wrote that God made the woman from Adam's "rib" (some say the Hebrew word really means "a cell") and presented her to the man.

What we need to understand is that God made a second human being, not just for Adam to marry, but in order that he would *not be alone*. Therefore, *you* do not have to marry in order not to be alone — all you need not to be alone is to have some other humans to be your companions and close friends.

A lot of people are not married and yet are not alone. So, we need to stop pressuring unmarried people to move into something that could prevent them from achieving the goal of total singleness. Marriage was not instituted, as you can see from God's attitude in Genesis 2, to solve the problem of being alone — human beings were created as an answer to that problem.

God "presented" Eve to Adam; in other words, at first He did not give Eve to Adam as a wife. Rather, He presented Adam with a companion just right for him. Adam was not alone in the sense of being without some kind of companionship.

Look at the verses just above where it says for every dog, there was a dog; for every fish, there was a fish; for every bird, there was a bird; but for the man, there was not another like him.

Eve was not created primarily as a wife but as *another like Adam*, who would first be a companion; then, later, a wife. All you need not to be alone is to find someone else like you, and there are around five billion people like you on earth today. You do not need to marry all of them — or any of them — in order not to be alone. You just need to be a companion with some of them.

Marriage will not solve "aloneness." Many people are married now, and the marriages are not working. They pray to get free, sleep in separate beds, operate in tension in the home. Marriages like that create more aloneness. Many of them are so miserable it is like living in torment — yes, in hell — all the time. Marriage is not the answer to being alone.

If you have been taught to operate in faith, do not be too quick to "claim" a specific person as husband or wife.

God Only *Presents*; You Choose

You will notice in Genesis the true pattern of God is that *God presented* the woman to the man. You may pray for a husband or wife, but then wait for God to present him or her.

It is essential to note that God only presented her to the man. He did not choose her for the man. He preserved man's power to choose by simply presenting her. Adam made the decision. He *chose* her. In essence, God will not choose your mate for you; for, if He did, that would violate your will and power of choice.

As a matter of fact, if God chose your mate for you, He would not only be violating your right to choose, but He would be taking responsibility for your relationship. If it failed, the blame could be transferred to God. This point is crucial, for I have counseled many individuals who were misguided by the misconception that God has created only one specific person on this planet for them to marry.

Think about the danger of such thinking. That means the odds are one to five billion for you to find that "right" one. Others have gone so far as to use prophecy to justify this misconception.

If God will, and has, chosen one individual out of the five billion on the planet just for you, and did it without your knowledge and permission (and without the other person's), then why would He not *choose* salvation for you? That is a much more vital area of your life. If God would violate our rights to choose in a temporary, earthly relationship, why not in an eternal, heavenly relationship with Himself?

God expresses His limitation on your will in His heart's sentiment that **"I wish that none would perish, but that all would come to repentance."** (2 Pet. 3:9.)

Because He chose to give man the right to choose, He has limited Himself to only expressing His wishes for us, not *making* us fulfill His wishes. Therefore, if God will not even choose eternal life for you, how much less will He choose a temporary earthly partner for you.

No, in regard to choosing a lifetime mate, you must understand that *you* have the power of choice to exercise among many individuals that life will *present* to you. Whether or not you use the Word, wisdom, and characteristics of God's nature to make that choice, you must take the responsibility for your choice — and for all the consequences that come with it.

Do not become overly spiritual, "spooky," or irrational in this regard. Remember the old saying, "Whatever bed you choose, you must also sleep in it."

Providing prospects is God's responsibility, but choosing a mate is yours. Rely on the assistance of the Holy Spirit, but do not attempt to transfer the responsibility of choice to Him.

What Does *Alone* Mean?

When God said it was not good for Adam to be *alone*, the word used has three major foundational definitions: "exclusive, isolated, solitary."

Suppose we read what God said according to those definitions:

"It is not good for man to be exclusive."

"It is not good for man to be isolated."

"It is not good for man to be in a solitary state."

To summarize God's view of singleness, I want to use an illustration of a key ring and a bunch of keys. If you have one, get it out and look at it. Each key is unique, separate, and whole, yet all of the keys are joined by a common ring. The keys are single, but not alone; thus it is possible to be single and not alone.

God did *not* say it was not good for man to be unique, separate, or whole.

As a matter of fact, God likes uniqueness so much that He did not allow two human beings out of all of the billions who have lived to have identical fingerprints. In addition, there are other things about human beings which are never replicated in other human beings, such as eye retina patterns, DNA cells, or the sperm content of men.

Our conclusion must be that God not only likes uniqueness, separateness, and wholeness, He *insists* on it in His creations.

It is therefore vital for you to understand that being single — "separate, unique, and whole" — is most essential to, and the foundation of, not only marital relationships but all relationships. I admonish you to consider how much you have refined your separateness from others, uniqueness to others, and your wholeness for others. Remember, a relationship is only as good as whatever the individuals involved bring to it. The omelet is only as good as the eggs in it.

*"Singleness is a state
to be pursued, not avoided.
To be single should be the
goal of every married person."*

2

God Wants You To Be Single

If you are able to catch hold of this revelation of the difference between being single and being alone, you will never again despise the state of being unmarried. Also, you will not marry, or encourage others to marry, based on wrong reasons.

The Church today is suffering from confusion among young and old, divorced and widowed, and those who are unhappily married because of misunderstanding this concept. Many pastors and congregations pressure unmarried people in their churches to stop being alone, when the people have not yet achieved the state of being single! The result is more unhappy marriages and more divorces.

The primary thing you need to understand from Scripture is that when God observed that it was not good for Adam to be alone, Adam was totally whole (Eve was taken out of him), totally unique, and totally separate. He did not even know he needed someone else.

Until you get to that state, you are not ready to stop being alone.

In other words, God said, "It is not good for a man to be alone *if he is single.*"

That means, you do not need to marry someone until *you* are truly a single person. You are better off alone, if you are not yet single — if you are not yet unique, separate, and whole.

After God presented (gave, put on display) Eve to Adam, then Adam chose to take her and to give himself to her. At that stage, Adam was qualified to give himself away.

If you do not know who you are yet, what are you going to give to someone else?

If you do not know how much of a single person you are, how much are you going to give someone else?

The most dangerous thing in the area of marriage is for a sick person to marry a sick person. Therefore, it is more important to be "single" than to be married. I will even make a stronger statement: It is *safer* to be unmarried than married, if you are not yet single.

Some people believe that when you marry, you have solved the problem of being alone. However, some of the loneliest people in the world are in marriages. Loneliness is magnified when you marry, if you are not unique, separate, and whole, or if your spouse is not.

There is no one so alone as a lonely married person, because he or she is trapped. The feeling of being trapped magnifies the loneliness. So it is much safer to be lonely unmarried, if you are going to be lonely.

Many people have thought, and still think, that getting married is the key to happiness. God has shown me that becoming whole and finding out your uniqueness is the real key to happiness. *And God has that key.*

Many have set marriage and "living happily ever after" as their goal in life. That is not the goal given us in the Word for a Christian's life.

The Goal of a Christian

The goal of a child of God is to become the separate, unique, and whole person the Lord wants you to become, the vessel that will hold the Treasure, which is Jesus. (2 Cor. 4:7.) The goal of each of us, according to the Apostle Paul, is "to be conformed to the image" of Christ (Rom. 8:29), Who was the most unique, separate, and whole person Who ever lived.

Whether you are aware of the goal, whether you are working toward it, or whether you are not, that still is the goal set before each of us.

We cannot rightly carry out the Great Commission (Mark 16:15-18) or be "perfected" to do the work of the ministry (Eph. 4:12) unless we have first achieved — or at least are working toward achieving — the goal of becoming a whole and unique child of God, conformed to the image of Christ.

Therefore, you should be striving to be single; however, *if you have married on the way to this goal,* do not stop seeking the goal. Marriage will simply show how "unsingle" you are.

Once I was in Germany at one of the largest rehabilitation centers (mental institutions) in Europe talking to the chief physician.

I said, "Do you know what is the problem of all of these people in here?"

He said, "Yes, we've studied that."

I said, "No, let me give you my definition of their *problem.* If you knew the problem, you could have the answer of why this place stays so full of patients. The problem is that everyone is trying to find his or her person in someone else's body. They are not 'single.' "

Women suffer more than men from the "myth of singleness." Society, even with the prominence of the

19

feminist movement today, tends to look down on, to set apart, women who are not married — especially those who have never married.

The thought seems to be that, if a woman has never married, it is because no one ever wanted her, which makes her a "reject," suspicious. There must be something wrong with her.

Many women and men are so busy looking for someone to be all things to them that they do not have time to be who they are. If you are too preoccupied looking for someone to be all things to you, you will have no one and nothing to give them.

Then you have a major problem in the making, because no one can ever give you enough time or attention to make up for the emptiness where you are supposed to be full. And if you are empty of a real self, the other person will be unhappy because you have nothing to give back.

If you will become consumed with being who you are, God will have to interrupt you to bring you a companion, just as He did Adam. Adam was so busy naming the animals, taking dominion (rulership) over the earth, and carrying out the functions he was created to perform that he did not have time to know there was not another one like him.

He was so consumed with enjoying life in the Garden of Eden, in fulfilling his purpose, that he did not look around for anyone else. God had to interrupt Adam and put him to sleep in order to make another like him to present to him.

Adam did not know he needed someone. And when you get to the point that you do not need anyone else for your life to be whole, unique, and separate, then you will be ready for God to bring you someone. You will be ready to give up your aloneness in favor of togetherness with someone else who is separate, whole, and unique.

Your marriage will only be as successful as your singleness, because you can only bring to a marriage what you are as a person alone. Marriage is honorable in itself. It is what we bring into it that causes the trouble.

No human being can meet your ego needs.

No human being can meet your soul needs.

No human being can meet your spiritual needs.

You might as well settle all that with God. *You are only fit, or ready, for marriage when you are totally fulfilled in God.*

You Must Love Yourself

Before you love others, you must love yourself. I am not talking about self-centeredness or self-love, pride or selfishness. I am talking about finding out who you are in Christ *and* as a person, then coming to terms with that person. Knowing who you are is the first step toward wholeness, and accepting that person is the second step.

In all the troubled marriages I have counseled over the past fifteen years, I have found that, generally, those marriages are made up of two self-haters trying to love one another.

If you need to get married to be fulfilled or loved, you are not ready for marriage. The very thing that makes you need to get married will become the problem in the marriage.

In Matthew 22:39, Jesus told the people to love their neighbors as themselves. You cannot love your neighbor if you do not love yourself.

People "fake one another out" with false hugs and kisses in church. They appear to be so loving — when they hate themselves.

"God bless you, pastor. I love you."

I do not want any "God bless you's" from people who do not even like themselves.

The next time someone says to you, "I love you," try answering, "But do you love *you*?"

It is not important whether you say you love me. This thing is not going to work until you love *you*, because if you do not love you, you are going to be looking to me to make up for that. You are going to expect from me more than I can possibly give in order to make up for what you lack in yourself.

The Word of God is so simple, and we can make it so confusing. We get so busy trying to love our neighbors that we have no time to love ourselves. Then we get disappointed in ourselves and add to self-rejection when we find we cannot love *them*.

Most of the time, we project the blame onto them. We gossip, judge, criticize, and all the time, we are really thinking badly of ourselves. The more they look bad to us, the better we look to ourselves. So we are building ourselves up at their expense.

You have to think you are better than other people in order to judge them. Thinking you are better is not loving yourself. Most of the time, it is covering up hate.

I love myself when I go to a meeting, and I love myself when I leave. I do not need anyone else to love me, because I am a whole person. I enjoy people liking me. I enjoy the love of my wife. I enjoy companionship and not being alone. But I am never lonely, even when I am by myself.

I know it is tough being unmarried in a world designed for couples. Have you ever gone into a restaurant and seen a chair by itself at a table? Everyone assumes there will be at least two people.

But being conformed by the pressure of the world to its image will not make you happy. It is better to walk alone in an alien society than to be miserable with someone else just out of conformity to this world's standards.

Complete people are interesting to me. People who have vision, goals, purposes, and plans for their lives attract me. A whole person knows who he is, why he is at a certain place, where he is going, and how he is going to get there.

I believe this concept should be taught in all Christian schools, so children can grow up with the right ideas about themselves. My ministry, Bahamas Faith Ministries International, is helping develop a curriculum for the Third World people in our region.

We have formed an association called ''The Third World Christian Education Association.'' We are examining the problems in the foundation of the curricula of our present schools that result in the system's turning out young people who hate themselves.

Jesus said the greatest commandment is to love God with your whole heart, and the second greatest is to love your neighbor to the same degree you love yourself. (Luke 10:27.)

That means the key is loving you, not other people. You can only love people to the extent that you accept and love yourself.

*"A successful marriage is only
the product of two people being
successfully single."*

3

The Advantage of Being Unmarried

God originally made mankind as singles, both in the sense of "unmarried," and in the sense of being "separate, unique, and whole."

I believe one of the most important messages the Lord wants the Church to have in these years is this: Being unmarried is the highest calling in the realm of relationships.

That is because a successful marriage is only the product of two people being successfully single. If you are not yet successful at being single — if you cannot control your emotions, your passions, your feelings, your attitudes and behavior — then you are not prepared for marriage.

Today, God is saying, "Please get your act together as an unmarried person. Get your standards and values settled. Build yourself on the Rock, Christ Jesus, and set your feet on the bedrock of the Word so that pressures of the world will not move you."

Some Christians are falling to the temptations of the world like flies attracted to honey, because their feet are not planted on the Word.

I have found from reading history that some of the greatest contributions to the Kingdom have been made by unmarried persons. Let me give you some examples:

*The late Corrie ten Boom of Holland, world evangelist, never married. She and her family saved many Christians and Jews from the Nazis and spent year in German prison camps when they were caught. Her talks and books after World War II brought millions to the Lord.

Her book, *The Hiding Place*, has been made into a movie that also touched millions. Her whole life was bound up in God. She was truly single and singleminded.

I met her many times, and each time I saw her, I wanted to be near her. You could feel the anointing of the Holy Spirit when you came near her. I felt as if I were in the presence of God.

Once in Tulsa, Oklahoma, she said to me, "Don't be so preoccupied with who you aren't, for you may forget who you are. Don't get sidetracked by the devil so that your main goal is to find a mate. Get preoccupied with God."

*C. S. Lewis, perhaps the greatest apologist of the Christian faith in our day, was unmarried during all the years he was writing his books. He did marry a few years before he died, but the main work of his life was over by then. His writings have influenced millions to become Christians or to become better Christians. (*Apologist* does not mean "apologizing for," but "explaining or defending" the faith.)

*Martin Luther was single, focused on God, when he made his great discovery of justification by faith in the Bible, thus restoring personal salvation to the Church. However, he also married later.

*John Calvin, one of the great men of the Reformation, was unmarried.

*The Apostle Paul, to go back to Bible days, was unmarried to say nothing of Jesus Himself. Without Paul's total focus on Jesus with his spirit, soul, *and* body, we would not have almost half the New Testament. Without Paul's singleness, we probably would not understand as well the teachings of Jesus or the connections between the Old and New Covenants.

*Many of the Old Testament prophets, such as Ezekiel, Daniel, Elijah, and Elisha did not marry.

Paul wrote in First Corinthians 7:32,33 that unmarried people are free to be concerned only with the things of God, while a married person has divided interests and cannot be totally focused on God.

However, please note that he also said not everyone was "called" to the state of remaining unmarried. (1 Cor. 7:7.) In other words, not everyone can live unmarried for a lifetime.

In that case, Paul said, "Better get married." (1 Cor. 7:9.)

Seek First the Kingdom

If you are yet unmarried, and you know you do not want to live in that state for the rest of you life, now is the time to become truly single so that your marriage will be successful in God.

The best promise in the Word on which to stand, in case you do choose to marry is Matthew 6:33:

> **But seek ye first the kingdom of God, and His righteousness; and all these things shall be added unto you.**

The average lifespan today is about 70 years. So if you marry between 20 and 30, you have 40 to 50 years to live in the state of marriage. Most people think life begins with marriage, but what do they do in the first period to prepare for "the rest of their lives"?

Marriage is like building a house. Marrying without first being single would be like spending years putting up walls, then putting on a roof, adding doors and windows, and so forth, but finding out, finally, that you have forgotten to build a foundation. That marriage is built on sand, and it will topple, sooner or later. You should build *you* before building a marriage.

"Is it not better, however,
to begin with <u>two</u> good eggs?"

4

An Omelet Is Only as Good
as the Eggs

Whether you understand what I am saying or not, this is a fact: an omelet is only as good as the eggs that are in it. If there is one rotten egg, it will spoil the whole omelet. How good the other egg is will not make any difference.

And you cannot separate an omelet into eggs again. However, not to carry that analogy too far, God can change a "rotten egg" into a good one and reconstruct the omelet (marriage). But He is the only One Who can do it.

Is it not better, however, to begin with two good eggs?

Proverbs 25:28 is pregnant with truth and life. This verse has the answers to what we are discussing.

> He that hath no rule over his own spirit is like a city
> that is broken down, and without walls.

To bring that principle into modern terms, let me paraphrase it:

"He who does not have full control of himself (or herself), is like an open city for anyone to take over and rule."

Or we might say, "Anyone who does not know who he or she is becomes fair game for someone else to mold into another image."

Jesus taught this in Matthew 13. In verse 3, He began to tell a story, a parable, of sowing seeds into different kinds of ground. The disciples, being as intelligent and quick to understand as most of us, did not understand a word He said. After the meeting, they asked Him to explain — which He did.

He talked about four kinds of "soil," but I only want to draw one of them to your attention: that of the stony ground. In verse 21, Jesus said the reason people with that kind of heart cannot stand when persecution comes is because *they have no roots in themselves.*

The root of any plant is its source of nutrients, the source of strength, the source of the shape that plant takes and the fruit it bears. Jesus was saying those people without enough of the Word in them, those people who are not yet "separate, whole, and unique" because of being founded on Him, have no roots in themselves.

Churches today are filled with people dying in the midst of life, people who have no roots in themselves. Other people's opinions of them are more important to them than the way they think of themselves. On the other extreme, people who are so full of pride and self-importance that other people's reactions to them do not count have just as many broken walls under all that facade.

Jesus did not need anyone else's opinion to verify Who He was. He knew Who He was. Until you become whole, you will always be dependent on other people's opinions for your self-worth.

The middle ground is to be so whole in your uniqueness that you can respect other people's opinions but not be moved if people do not see you rightly or try to mold you into their patterns.

Marriage Is Not 50-50

We have been taught that marriage is a 50-50 proposition, which is a doctrine from the pit of hell. If marriage is 50-50, each person is only half a person. Marriage is like an omelet made from two good, whole eggs, not two half-eggs.

If you have a 50-50 marriage, you have two persons, each half-whole. Then you have a problem! They spend the rest of their lives together trying to steal from each other what is needed for wholeness — uniqueness, personality, things that make the other special.

In other words, in that kind of marriage, one or both partners are empty. Adam was totally whole. Eve was totally whole. When God said Eve was "meet" or suitable for Adam, He meant she could "fit or adapt to" him. She was his equal.

In most marriages today, both parties spend years trying to change the other into a clone of themselves or to fit the image they have in their minds of what a husband or wife should be.

I am one hundred percent me. My wife is one hundred percent herself. I do not *need* her to make me whole, and she does not *need* me to make her whole. I looked for a wife who would not need me to make her whole, because I have too many things to do for the Lord to spend time dealing with an empty or half-empty wife.

May the Lord bring into your spirit the knowledge that all you need to stop being alone is another human being, not a husband or wife.

Loneliness Is a Disease

Solomon said, "He who would have friends must be friendly." (Prov. 18:24.)

That means, if you are lonely, it is because you are not a friendly person. If you are lonely, you are "sick," because God created man to be whole in his aloneness, not lonely, not yearning for someone else to make him whole.

If you are lonely, find someone else who is alone (not half-empty) and make friends. Begin to reach out to others who are unmarried like yourself. There are people by the hundreds in churches who stand in the congregations, lift their hands to praise and worship, but stand in loneliness and go home lonely.

Loneliness is a sickness that comes from not understanding who you are and from being afraid or too proud to make close friends. A person whose "walls" are whole and intact can feel safe in opening doors to others for companionship.

You can tell whether you are a whole person by how well you keep company with yourself. Some people are afraid to be alone. They always want other people around, because they do not like themselves, or they are so empty they have to live through others.

When these people are home alone, they have the radio or television on or watch a video, or perhaps they read, because their emptiness must be filled with something or somebody outside themselves.

On the other hand, an attitude of isolation and of being a "hermit" is a sign of a different kind of sickness. Both extremes are evidence of a person who is not yet whole and unique, not yet really single.

A happily married man or woman is still single. The problem is that we are all born empty, and some of the junk with which we have filled ourselves should not be there.

No one was born to be married; however, everyone was born not to be alone. There is no special anointing that comes with marriage.

Nowhere in the Bible does the Lord say, "Thou shalt marry."

Every human being is a "help meet" for every other human being. Every person you meet keeps you from being alone. Out of all of the thousands you probably will see or meet in your lifetime, you can ask God to choose one to present to you as a permanent help-meet.

Please do not misunderstand. God does not *choose* for you. That would violate your will. However, if you ask Him, He will bring along one that He knows is suitable for you to choose. Also, if you submit your will to Him and ask Him to choose, He will. But He will not force anyone on you. In the final analysis, your spouse must be of your choosing — either to pick or to accept — or the marriage will not work.

There is a lot of presumption going around in the church world today in all areas. In the area of marriage, a number of these presumptions are particularly dangerous:

1) "Claiming" a particular person without finding out God's opinion.

2) "Prophesying" So-and-so is to marry So-and-so. Usually, that is wishful thinking, or someone else trying to impose his thinking on you. In some cases, it is even a trap set for you by Satan.

3) Going around telling a girl or a guy, "God told me you are going to marry me." Usually, the person who says this is trying to manipulate the other person into marriage. That is spiritualizing foolishness.

If you are unmarried and find yourself attracted to someone else, you had better find out why very quickly. It could be sensual; it could be that you feel that person fills an empty area in you; it could be you are feeling the pressure of the world to get married.

*"A person in a state of being
single is a joy to the Lord."*

5

Singleness Is God's Joy

Being unmarried is not a curse, and singleness is the first blessing of man. A person in a state of being single is a joy to the Lord. When God can deal with a person who is whole and unique, He can get more done.

I believe that is why God made Adam first. He wanted an individual, a single-minded person, who would be filled with Him. I believe people like the Apostle Paul who find such fulfillment in being unmarried in the Lord are a special joy to God. He has a special feeling for those who are satisfied and fulfilled with Him alone. He can do more through them.

This state of being unmarried, however, has to be a choice, a total dedication of yourself to God. It is not blessed if it is forced on you by others, even by religious institutions. In other words, I am not saying that everyone should become a monk or a nun. Paul included "forbidding to marry" in his list of doctrines of devils. (1 Tim. 4:3.)

My wife and I do not regret marrying; however, there are things we cannot do for the Lord now that we could have done as unmarried workers. We regret not being able to do those things. However, marriage is wonderful, but it is not necessary for everyone's personal fulfillment.

Paul wrote that if you marry, it is not a sin. However, in essence, he wrote to the Corinthian church that "those who marry have many troubles I do not have." (1 Cor. 7:32,33).

Unmarried Christians should be so consumed by God and His will, so preoccupied and committed to finding out who they are in Him, that they are not distracted by the search for other people. You can spend so much time looking for who you want that you have no time to be who you are.

Amen!!

Singleness is a joy, and marriage is a joy; but, all of the time I am married, I do not ever want to stop being a single, whole person.

Remember, God did not create marriage first. Yet, the Church many times has taught, at least by implication, that being unmarried is a sin. If God made singleness of first importance, if He used it as the first block in building humanity, then we need to take a look at what is involved in that revelation.

We have been saying that marriage is the building block of society. But that is not what God thought. He thought two single people, whole and entire in themselves, were the building blocks of humanity. Marriage is simply two single people. You do not become a Siamese twin when you marry; you are not suddenly half of someone else.

Mankind Was Built on Individuals

Biblical marriage is two wholes becoming one, which is much stronger than two halves becoming one. If society is built on marriage, then what is marriage built on? If it is built on one or two rotten eggs, you have a rotten omelet, as I wrote earlier.

God created humanity and a world that began with an individual. Marriage is important for the *survival* of humanity; however, God *built* humanity on individuals.

Those who are married should realize that the only thing that binds them together is a covenant. You are the same old you, and your spouse is the same person he or she was before you married. That marriage contract, or covenant, is only as good as your word, your promise to keep it.

Without the Holy Spirit, it is almost impossible to have a successful and happy marriage. He provides the power to enable you to keep your vows. The world has a saying that promises are made to be broken. Without the Holy Spirit, you would make promises you could not keep.

God designed everything in the Kingdom around the individual, beginning with salvation. He never saves groups, only individuals. One of Billy Graham's London crusades resulted in about a million people making commitments to Jesus Christ.

However, God did not scoop up those million people in a great big Holy Spirit shovel and dump them in the ocean of the blood of Jesus. No, each one sat in a single seat, heard the Word singly, and the Holy Spirit came to each and saved him individually as he received Jesus. Each got out of his or her seat, personally, and walked to the front to confess Jesus.

They stood together in large groups, but that mass was made up of individuals all making individual choices. That is the way God works. Even when the disciples were baptized in the Holy Spirit on the Day of Pentecost (Acts 2), God did not send just one tongue. He sent tongues of fire on each one, and the Holy Spirit sat on each, individually.

The word *disciple* is more important to God than *spouse*, because a disciple is an individual follower of Jesus. If every unmarried Christian would realize that becoming God's single person would be such a joy to Him, perhaps we would have more committed Christians. Also, we would have more people allowing themselves to be prepared by God for the state of marriage.

*"Most people do not get prepared;
they just get married."*

6

Prepared for Marriage

As I have said, marriage is what I call "the second level of God's building blocks." There came a time, after the Lord had revealed this concept to me, that He began to prepare me for marriage.

The way He did that was to lead me into being so consumed with becoming who He had made me, that I did not have time to worry, or wonder or build fantasies about the woman God was preparing to present to me as a help meet.

Marriage is necessary to fulfill God's purposes, but it is not necessary to fill the place the Church and the world have assigned it — to take two halves and make a whole. And to choose God instead of a spouse is still a higher calling, but do not choose the life of single-minded focus on Jesus unless you are positive you can do it and that an unmarried lifestyle is His will for you.

If you choose an unmarried life out of religious pressure, or false spirituality, or being "disappointed in love," then you are not giving God a whole, truly single person. You will be cheating Him and yourself.

If you know the unmarried life is not for you, then begin to ask God to prepare you for marriage. Ask Him to help you become a whole person, not a half person, or a leech.

Do Not Be a Leech

Sometimes when I am counseling people with marital problems, they begin to say things out of their hurt, such as:

"If she leaves me, I won't be able to make it."

"If he leaves me, my whole life will fall apart. Who is going to do this, and who is going to do that? Who is going to take care of the children and pay the rent? We'll lose the house and the car," and so forth.

Many people begin to "attach" themselves to their husbands or wives instead of allowing God to bond them together. Soon, they have "become" the other person's and feel they cannot live without them.

I do not *want* to become my wife, and she does not want to become me! We are two *single* people bonded together by God in a marriage covenant. Each of us has remained a unique individual.

The world thinks of romance in terms like, "I don't exist without you," or "I can't get along without you," or "If you go away, my world goes." That is not romantic! That is addictive dependency. Instead of an addictive substance, you are addicted to a person.

I did not *get* married; I was prepared for marriage. God prepared me for 25 years for the marriage that was within His purpose for me.

Most people do not get prepared; they just get married.

Have you prepared yourself for marriage as a single individual?

Have you asked God to prepare you?

One thing you will learn as God prepares you for marriage is not ever to lose yourself. Do not slip into "losing yourself" in someone else. You will be "sucking" life from them, or they will be taking life from you.

Individuality is important to God. That means being able to be yourself, have your own opinions and decisions, come up with your own ideas about things. You are not to lose your identity when you marry.

Christians want God's marriage product; but, many times, they do not want God's ingredient. What is God's ingredient in marriage? His ingredient is the same as it is in the life of an individual: His love.

God's Ingredient

Many Spirit-filled Christians like to read or to hear First Corinthians 13, ''the love chapter.'' They like hearing that ''love never fails,'' and love is this and that. The greatest sinner in the world likes that chapter.

''Oh, I want my marriage to be like that,'' they say. ''I want my marriage never to fail.''

The word for *love* in that chapter is the same word used in the list of the fruits of the Spirit (Gal. 5:22,23). That word is the Greek word *agape,* which means ''divine love,'' God's love.

Men want what love says it can give, but they do not want the Spirit Who brings it. They are trying to get a finished product without the right ingredients.

If you want God's love, you have to have God's Spirit, and if you want God's Spirit, you must receive God's Son, the Lord Jesus Christ.

Here is something else that may shock you: sinners are not joined together by God. I will discuss this more in the next chapter.

God's ingredient that ensures a happy marriage is not available without taking Jesus with it.

Romans 5:5 does not say, ''The love of God is shed abroad in our hearts by watching television or movies or by reading magazines.''

Paul did not write that the love of God is shed abroad in our hearts by going to college. His love does not come into our hearts by kissing and caressing one another.

That verse does not even say, "The love of God comes into our hearts by reading or hearing the Word." *Faith* comes by hearing the Word.

God's love "is shed abroad in our hearts *by the Holy Spirit,*" the Apostle Paul wrote. So without His love being brought into our hearts by the Holy Spirit, God cannot guarantee a finished product of a happy marriage. He cannot guarantee two sinners eternal love.

Marriage in God's Context

So, singleness is the first state in which God made you, and marriage is for those who are able to carry it out in God's context, according to Jesus. (Matt. 19:3-12.)

What *is* God's context? His plan and His context for marriage is *permanence.* Not everyone is ready for marriage, according to Jesus in that teaching to His disciples and the Pharisees recorded in Matthew 19.

He was saying, "If you cannot handle permanence in marriage, then as a believer, don't get into it. However, if you are able to handle it, go ahead."

That is why the disciples answered, "If this is true, it is not good to marry!" (v. 10.)

Get prepared by yourself, so you know for certain that, no matter what comes — storms, floods, the deepest valleys, or the highest mountains — you will be able to make it by yourself. Then you will be the kind of person prepared to receive the marriage vow.

*"The only people God puts
together are two people with
the Holy Spirit within them.
Everyone else, man marries."*

7

We Live in Two Worlds

As long as Christians are physically alive, they exist in two different worlds: one is material and still under the influence of the satanic world system. The other is supernatural, eternal, and the *real* world which is under the authority of God.

Whether we intend it that way, or whether we even know it, we are influenced by the society, culture, and traditions of the natural world in which we live as much as we are by the political, economic, and educational systems.

The society of the natural world today thinks that if you are single, you are not normal. That thought has been planted in our subconscious minds from the time we were children. Most of the time, people are not consciously aware that is how they think.

Pressure to marry comes from all sides — from friends, enemies, family, society at large, and from cultural and news media. Even in advertisements on television, you can see pressure applied, although unintentional.

You will see a wife and a husband with a little boy brushing his teeth with this "special, wonderful, different" toothpaste. The conclusion is that you have to be married with a family for this toothpaste to really work. That is an oversimplified example, but certainly illustrates the point.

Society looks at an unmarried person more than 25 years old and thinks, "My, there must be something really wrong with him or her."

Practically everything in our society is constructed to make us think that, almost as soon as a person is born, he must begin to think about marrying. In some Asian cultures, even into modern times, children were betrothed to one another by their parents. Not only was marriage a foregone conclusion, but so was the marriage partner! No choices. That is bondage and interferes with man's God-given "right to choose."

You will see youngsters of 12 and 13 thinking in terms of "boyfriend" and "girlfriend." By 14, they think there is something wrong with them if they do not have love interests.

Sometimes a parent will get upset with a child this age and say, "What are you doing, wanting to go out with this boy (or girl)? You are still a child. Don't try to grow up too fast," and so forth.

What the parents do not realize is that during all of that child's life, they have been subconsciously feeding the marriage concept into his mind.

The information received by that child is this: "Being unmarried is bad. It is weird. You will not be happy unless you marry. The world will make fun of you unless you marry. You will be a misfit."

Also, adulthood is connected to marriage in our thinking. The feeling is that in order to be grown up, you must marry. That is a necessary part of adult life. So, even unmarried adults feel they are less than "human."

Married couples usually do not invite unmarried people to their parties or dinners, at least not by themselves. They will invite an unattached man for an unmarried female, and vice versa. Many times, very quickly, the unmarried female will not be invited at all, a sad situation.

If being unmarried means being "sub-human," then God created sub-humans, because He made us first of all to be "single, unique, whole, separate-from-any-other, unmarried beings." However, as the Lord has shown me, and as I hope you have seen by now, God did not create sub-humans, but whole, single humans.

Divorce Is of This World

You are not a "whole, single" being who is prepared for marriage until you are prepared never to get a divorce. You are not ready to marry until you reach the understanding that marriage, in God's context, as we said in the last chapter, is permanent.

In Matthew 19, Jesus was separating the two worlds. The Pharisees asked Him a question:

Is it lawful for a man to put away his wife for every cause (v. 3)?

"Every cause" really meant "any cause," and that covers a lot of territory. The Pharisees thought they were putting Jesus on the spot with that question. However, He immediately began to separate the two worlds.

He said, ...**Have ye not read, that he which made them at the beginning made them male and female** (v. 4)?

The first thing He did was refer them back to creation. They knew the Old Testament as well as He did, and better than most of us do today. Those Pharisees knew immediately what He was talking about.

In Genesis 1 and 2, we are looking at God's world. That is where the man and the woman were created. Jesus was telling them that God's world is the first world. Then in Genesis 3, Adam and Eve fell, and suddenly, we see the second world, one under the influence of Satan.

In the beginning, man and woman were righteous, walking in harmony with God, and fellowshipping with God in the cool of the day. They were at one with God.

After the fall, there was no fellowship and oneness with God as formerly. There was no covenant as yet: only God's promise of a Deliverer to come who would bruise Satan's head. Also, there began to be division between the man and woman and between their children.

In chapter 3, the second world has come into existence. The husband blamed the wife, and she blamed the serpent. In chapter 3, fear entered the second world, and the couple became ashamed and felt disgraced. In chapter 3, violence entered the second world, and the elder brother killed the younger.

The Pharisees knew that conditions in chapter 2 of Genesis were ideal and perfect, and that God joined man and woman in a context of permanence.

What they were asking Jesus was, "Can this condition of permanence be applied to everyone? Moses did not think so. So was God wrong, or was Moses wrong?"

They thought this "trick" question would put Jesus in the wrong, no matter how He answered. This is only one of several times they did this in His ministry, and they never caught Him in the wrong.

The Garden Experience

This time, Jesus pointed out that God's original creation and Moses' decree that allowed divorce were operating in two different worlds.

He said, "God made a male and a female, and He intended for a man to leave his parents and be joined permanently to his wife. After that, they will be two whole people joined into a oneness bigger than both of them." (v. 4-6.)

It was possible for a man and a woman who knew no sin to become totally one, and Jesus said, "When God puts a man and woman together, no man had better try to tear them apart." (v. 6b.)

However, Jesus was saying, "As far as I am concerned, the people in the world can legally marry and live together, but God did not marry them."

Christians today, new creatures born under a New Covenant between God and man, are supposed to be living in chapter 2 of Genesis. Relationship has been initiated. We have been adopted into the family of God. Fellowship has been restored between God and man, man and woman, and among mankind through the unity of the Holy Spirit.

The only people God "puts together" are two people who have the Holy Spirit within them. Everyone else, man marries.

Many non-Christians go to a church to get married "before God," and they go through a ceremony and through rituals. But the building is not where God lives.

His "building" today is the Church. His born-again children are individual temples of God. So, being married in a church building does not mean God has put that man and woman together.

If you really believe God put you and your spouse together, you have no right to go to a lawyer.

If you believe you married *in the Lord,* then you would have to go back to a preacher to get a divorce.

Try saying to him, as God's representative, "We want to get a divorce," and see what happens. As soon as you hit the church door, if not before, the Holy Spirit is going to say:

47

"I thought you, being My children, knew that the Father requires forgiveness of others so that He can forgive you." (Luke 6:37.)

If I am invited to a wedding (I am a covenant witness), and later that couple decides to divorce, I expect to be invited to witness the divorce just as I witnessed the wedding.

Two born-again people who marry are back in the Garden experience.

They have the Holy Spirit. They should be able to handle problems through love and forgiveness and through walking in the fruits of the Spirit. They are no longer two, but one.

Was Moses Wrong?

I will not marry two unbelievers. I cannot do it. God is not in it. Neither will I marry a believer to an unbeliever and sanctify by the Word an unequally yoked couple. (2 Cor. 6:14.)

If two unbelievers are already married, and one of them comes to God, that is a different situation, which the Apostle Paul covers in First Corinthians 7:14. I am talking about officiating at a marriage, not dealing with situations that arise after marriage.

Then the Pharisees asked Jesus, "Well, okay, what about Moses? Are you saying that the father of our law was wrong?"

Jesus said, "No, I am saying that Moses *had* to allow divorce, because Israel was living in the second world and their hearts were hardened, just as yours are today."

Moses faced a rough situation. As "president," so to speak, over some three and a half million basically pagan people living in a wilderness, he had to rule over them and keep them as close to righteous living as he could.

If you read Exodus, you will see some of the abominable sexual sins that were prevalent. Otherwise, God would never have handed down commandments against incest, bestiality, homosexuality, and so forth. It would not have been necessary.

Divorce was not a commandment from God. It was a decree from Moses.

Jesus said, "Divorce was Moses' idea, not God's. It was not God's plan, but Moses allowed it for the sake of peace in the nation and peace in families. He *had* to because of the hardness of your hearts."

Moses said, "These people are full of sin, so to avoid having a massacre of husbands and wives, let's come up with a bill allowing them to separate. At least, we'll survive as a nation."

Today, those who are filled with the Holy Spirit are not even supposed to have the word *divorce* in their vocabulary. It is an unthinkable thought in God's world.

There is only one cause for breaking apart a marriage in God's world, and that is fornication, Jesus said. (Matt. 19:9.) Fornication is like murder to God, because it is a direct assault on the physical temple of God.

If you are an unbeliever, you can get a divorce anytime. Many times, divorce is a blessing to an unbeliever. But it is a curse to believers. To the believer, divorce is not even up for discussion. God is not in the marriages of unbelievers in the first place. Their "father" is Satan, and they are of the kingdom of darkness.

If you want the Garden experience, then you have to use the Garden system. Do you have one eye on God and the other on the girls or the guys? Then you are not totally whole yet. When both eyes are single-mindedly focused on the Kingdom of God and His righteousness, then God will say:

"*Now*, I see that it is not good for him, or her, to be alone. It is time for marriage."

*"True love is not a feeling;
it is a choice and a decision."*

8

Remain in the Station
Where God Called You

In First Corinthians 7:20, the Apostle Paul wrote, **Let every man abide in the same calling wherein he was called.**

Calling means "station" or "place" or "situation" where you were when you became born again. Paul explained:

For he that is called in the Lord, being a servant, is the Lord's freeman: likewise also he that is called, being free, is Christ's servant (v. 22).

In connection with marriage, the principle found in verse 22 means:

If you were not already married when you became born again, then continue in that state until you are a true single in the Lord before deciding to marry or not to marry.

However, if you were married when you became born again, that principle means *stay married*.

Do not read this book and go tell your husband or wife, "Honey, I have received a new revelation, and I am going to have to divorce you so I can start all over again. I have found out that singleness is the way to go first."

That is certainly *not* what I am saying!

If you are married, yet know from reading this book that you are not yet "single," then begin to seek God and

His Kingdom and ask Him to make you a whole, unique person *within* the context of your marriage.

If you are unmarried, do not desire to marry in order to learn who you are; if you are married, do not think you must become unmarried in order to learn.

Assets and Liabilities

Jesus and Paul taught, in essence, that marriage is permanent; therefore, marriage is only for those who can handle it. Jesus' words about being able to live alone as a single person imply that this is a "gift."

> **All men cannot receive this saying, save they to whom it is given** (this implies that it is a gift).

> **For there are some eunuchs, which were so born . . . some eunuchs, which were made . . . and there be eunuchs, which have made themselves eunuchs for the kingdom of heaven's sake.** *He that is able to receive it, let him receive it.*
> **Matthew 19:11,12**

Also, please note that *this is not a command.* You do not have to remain unmarried in order to minister. Jesus said to let those who are able choose to live this way. Everything is your choice. God will not override your will and make you an eunuch.

Paul also dealt with some assets and liabilities of each condition: unmarried and married.

In the climate of persecution that was intensifying, he said, an unmarried person would not have to deal with having a husband or wife dragged off and fed to the lions, or with leaving orphaned children behind, or with being pregnant in the gladiatorial ring.

On the other hand, in the promiscuous climate that co-existed with the brutal "circuses" for the Roman people, unmarried people were faced with more sexual temptation. The Corinthian church, especially, was in a society very similar to today's. Prostitutes, both male and female, were readily available. There were a lot of temples to Eros, the god of sex, in Corinth.

Today, Amsterdam, for example, has legal prostitution and streets with nothing but sex shops. In New York, there are places where, as a Christian, you feel you need to walk around with your eyes closed.

Paul said, "It's not a sin if you marry, but those who do will have physical and earthly troubles. Marriage has double trouble."

I have a happy marriage, a wonderful marriage. We think we have the best marriage in the world, but it would not be true to say there are not more challenges and more *responsibilities* than if we were both unmarried.

Marriage in God's context means making choices when you do not feel like it. *True love is not a feeling, it is a choice and a decision.*

Paul also pointed out that, in marriage, your body belongs to your spouse. When you were unmarried, you owned your body and could dedicate it totally to God. When you marry, you have no more exclusive authority over your body. (1 Cor. 7:3-5.)

The apostle said the only way a husband or wife can rightly deprive a spouse from sexual rights is if both mutually agree.

He said, do not *defraud* one another. That means "deprive, steal from, withhold from." There are many "thieves" who stand before God in church on Sunday morning, unaware that they are stealing from their spouses in the bedroom.

On the other hand, a marriage that is built on nothing but physical gratification will not last. That marriage is in trouble from day one.

I do pray that this revelation of what being *single* really means in God's Word and God's mind will help you become more like Jesus. Secondly, if you are married, or choose to marry, I pray this will help you improve the quality of your marriage and your life. I urge you to seek the Garden experience with God.

Remember that God began with a single, separate, unique, and whole individual totally preoccupied with God's purpose and assignment for his life. He did not seek after companionship. He was so preoccupied with his work that he was not aware he needed a mate.

The principle is this:

You are more effectively prepared for marriage when you do not need to be married. Your pursuit in life should not be marriage but *singleness*.

*"Do what you are called upon
to do wherever you are, and do
it as unto the Lord."*

9

Divorce and the Bible

The very word *divorce* brings as many reactions as there
are readers. I would venture to say that every person who
reads this book has been affected in one way or another
by the trauma of divorce.

If not personally experiencing one, you are from a home
of divorced parents, or someone in your family has gone
through this traumatic experience. Divorce is a condition
of society that has become increasingly common since World
War II.

So this part of the book is for those who have never
married, those who already are divorced, those who are
widows or widowers, and even those who believe they are
happily married.

Divorce is rampant in society today. Christians have
to face it and know *God's will* in various situations involving
divorce — not religious thinking.

Previously, in many of our cultures, even the word
divorce was taboo, much less the actual legal proceeding.
Somehow, today, divorce has become a normal part of life.

What is a *taboo*? That is something that you may know
exists, but you do not talk about. Most of the time,

something that is taboo is ignored. Even today, this is not a comfortable subject for Christians.

I am writing about separations as well, because separation is a divorce without legal papers. People can be "separated" and live in the same house, as we discussed in the first part of this book.

First, let us explore what the Bible has to say about divorce, what the world has to say about divorce, and what the devil is trying to do with divorce and separation.

Two people in the New Testament talked about divorce: Jesus and the Apostle Paul. To understand God's perspective on divorce, we have to know exactly what He said about it in His Word. When the two talked about marriage, they talked about divorce in the same verse or chapter.

Let us begin in Matthew 5:31, where Jesus is introducing the world to a new kingdom — a new government. So what He is dealing with in the Sermon on the Mount (Matt. 5, 6, and 7) are the changes in attitude and behavior necessary to live and function in the new kingdom.

He began with attitudes that we call "the Beatitudes." Then He talked about the fact that the new Kingdom, the Kingdom of heaven for which they had been looking, does not deal with outward appearances but with attitudes of the heart.

Jesus told His listeners that the Head of the Kingdom is God and that He deals with motives, not emotions. God is a heart-oriented God.

What Jesus Said

It hath been said, Whosoever shall put away his wife, let him give her a writing of divorcement:

But I say unto you, That whosoever shall put away his wife, saving for the cause of fornication, causeth her to

commit adultery: and whosoever shall marry her that is divorced committeth adultery.

Matthew 5:31,32

Then in Matthew 19, Jesus addressed the topic of divorce again. This time, His words were in response to questions from Pharisees.

And he answered and said unto them, Have ye not read, that he which made them at the beginning made them male and female,

And said, For this cause shall a man leave father and mother, and shall cleave to his wife: and they twain shall be one flesh?

Wherefore they are no more twain, but one flesh. What therefore God hath joined together, let not man put asunder.

Matthew 19:4-6

The Pharisees asked Him why Moses commanded men to give their wives certificates of divorce. They thought they had caught Jesus teaching against "the law of Moses."

Jesus told them that because of the hardness of their hearts, Moses allowed bills of divorcement, but reminded them that God did not create things that way. In essence, our present conditions are not God's original plan for man, and His ideal has become an ordeal.

His disciples understood that He was saying men could not put away their wives for every little thing as they had been able to since Moses' day. They understood Jesus was saying that only the breaking of a union through adultery or fornication was grounds for divorce.

No more walking out because she nagged, or could not cook, or someone else looked better, or had a better dowry. And the disciples thought if that was the case, then it was better not to marry! The causes for divorce in their day were trivial and multiple. Actually, the reason for a divorce was left to the judgment of the male.

Jesus said not everyone could live without marrying and yet without sinning sexually. Only three categories of people could live unmarried, He said. They were those who had been born without desire or without functioning sexual organs, those castrated by accident or on purpose — as many rulers did to slaves or captives in those days, or those who sacrificed natural desires to serve the Lord singlemindedly. (vv. 11,12.)

Jesus was saying marriage is not for everyone, nor is living alone for everyone. Marriage is not a requirement to serve God or to go to heaven. And marriage is not necessary to be a success in life.

The cultures and societies of most of the world have developed an attitude that marriage is a necessary evil, when it was intended to be a blessing. Not everyone can accept the commitment of marriage, and not everyone can accept the commitment of living single. Even a greater percentage of people are not prepared for this commitment spiritually, emotionally, physically, and materially.

What Paul Said

The Apostle Paul took what Jesus said and elaborated on it to the believers in Corinth, one of the most wicked cities of the time. Sexual immorality abounded. Corinth was a city of temples to various goddesses where the priestesses provided sex as part of the "worship" service to any man who brought the designated "offering."

One temple is reputed to have had as many as a thousand priestesses. Because this was part of their religious customs, priestesses were respected by the general public.

However, they were abhorred by the Jews, and Jewish believers carried over the same attitude, of course. But many of the non-Jewish people, and even some of the priestesses or former pagans, had become converted and were in the church, but not letting go of pagan customs.

Like many believers today, they had new hearts but the same old heads. Paul had to write several times (one letter apparently was lost to us) correcting them in several areas. The area of marriage and divorce was a major problem to them.

This was the church where a man was living with, or married to, his stepmother, for example. Because sex had been regarded as an open and public part of life, the attitude that one's sexual relationships were not only private but to be regulated by certain "rights" and "wrongs" was something Corinthians had trouble understanding and accepting.

So Paul was not addressing the subject by his own choice as to the entire Body of Christ, but in answer to requests from a specific local church for advice about some local situations. (1 Cor. 7:1.)

And the first thing he said was: **It is good for a man not to touch a woman!** (v. 1).

I expect they did not want to hear that. Now let us see what Paul meant. He did not leave anyone out but wrote advice — either the Lord's or his own — concerning every choice about marriage.

> **Nevertheless** *to avoid fornication,* **let every man have his own wife, and let every woman have her own husband.** (v. 2.)

Then he pointed out, however, that once you marry, *your body no longer belongs to you.* We talked about this in Chapter 8.

So, if you marry, he said, the first thing to realize is that your body is no longer yours. The second thing he points out about marriage (vv. 32-35) is: Once you marry, your time and attention are no longer your own.

Unmarried people can care solely about things that please the Lord, he said. But married people must care about things of the world and things that please one another.

If you have never been married, are divorced, or are widowed, I hope you get hold of this advice and consider it very, very carefully.

I hope I shake you out of casually or traditionally considering marriage. I hope you trip over this advice of Paul's before you reach the altar.

You need to say, ''Let me check myself to see if I have the right stuff to handle this person and this relationship until I die. It is safer to remain single than to get married, unless I am certain this is what I can do.''

In essence, are you willing to share your time, privacy, material goods, secrets, ambitions, dreams, goals, visions, and desires with another person? Marriage is the death and sacrifice of exclusivity on the altar of love.

Paul added that, if people cannot control themselves where sex is concerned, they had better marry to avoid fornication. (v. 2.) To deal with the problems of marriage is better than to ''burn with passion'' and fall into sin, he said. (v. 9.)

Once you activate the appetite of sex, there develops a hunger to be satisfied. The minute you experience sex in a real way, you have awakened something that will last until you are old. So be careful.

My advice is like Paul's: If you have not awakened your sexual appetite, do not do it. Spend your time and energy on the Lord and His work. Preoccupy yourself with preparations for the person God is preparing to present to you.

Paul's Advice to the Married

Suppose you are already married? Then Paul had some other advice:

*Let them not separate. (vv. 10,11.)

But, if they do, let them remain unmarried or let them be reconciled. (v. 11.)

*Even if you are married to an unbeliever, stay with him or her, if at all possible, for the sake of the children. (vv. 12-14.)

*If the unbeliever wants to leave, however, let him or her leave. In that case, you are not bound to them. (v. 15.) If the unbeliever is willing to adapt to the believer's new lifestyle, Paul is saying, then stay together.

If that person is willing to live with you and you are praying, reading the Bible, giving tithes, attending church, and ministering to the sick — then live with the unbeliever even if he or she does not immediately turn to God. You may win him or her by your example.

If you leave, that may have been God's only access to that unbeliever. The chances of the Holy Spirit reaching that person with salvation are much better if you remain. So live with them as long as possible.

Let means "to allow." That means if the unbeliever leaves, you *allow* him or her. Do not get in the way, do not stand in the door. Believers, do not run after them and grab their clothes. Do not call them every day wanting to know where they have been and what they have been doing — and who with! *Let them go!*

If you are hanging on to that spouse after he or she leaves, you are not obeying the Word. You might as well be trying to live in strife and contention over your beliefs.

Everyone who marries does not have perfect circumstances, unfortunately. There are times when the other person's will is involved. You might like to control it, but you cannot. That would be witchcraft.

Paul said, **God hath called us to peace** (v. 15). If every divorced person could understand this, he or she would begin to square their shoulders and lift their heads. The *peace* of the Holy Spirit keeps your mind on God and keeps you sane.

Paul gave these teachings in the context of remaining in whatever state you are when you get saved, as I talked about in Chapter 8. However, he was not talking about continuing to live in sin or still being a temple prostitute!

He was saying, ''Don't be weird. Don't get saved and go home and tell your husband or wife you can't sleep with him or her any longer because your body is the temple of God.

''If you are a slave bound to someone for years or for life, don't run away because you got saved. Stay, and be the best servant possible. Let God turn your circumstances. You keep your vows and do the right thing. (vv. 20-24.)

''If you are an employee, don't throw away your job to go sit 'in faith' and wait for God to drop something in your lap. Do what you are called upon to do wherever you are, and do it as unto the Lord.

''If you are a Jewish believer who was circumcised ritually on the eighth day, do not go to some Greek doctor and have another operation to cover that one up. (Many young men of the Jewish elite did just that when the Greek Olympic games — in which the participants were nude — became popular.)

''On the other hand,'' Paul said, ''if you are non-Jewish and have never been circumcised, don't go have it done now. That was the sign of the Old Covenant. Now your heart is circumcised in conversion as part of the New Covenant.''

Now, what about the unmarried virgins with whom Paul dealt? You may say, did he not already write about that when he wrote about the unmarried? No, he did not. *The unmarried* may be widows or widowers, divorced people, or those who have been sexually active without marriage.

That is why he addressed the situation of burning with passion. Look at verses 27 and 28:

> **Art thou bound unto a wife? seek not to be loosed. Art thou loosed from a wife? seek not a wife.**
>
> **But and if thou marry, thou hast not sinned. And if a virgin marry, she hath not sinned.** *Nevertheless such shall have trouble in the flesh . . . .*

Then Paul said, "I want to spare you this." Being a pastor of pastors, Paul must have had a deluge of requests to deal with problems. Based on all of the years of counseling experience I have had, I agree with Paul, although I love my wife. We have a happy marriage, but the principle remains: Alone, God can be your total focus. Married, your attention necessarily is divided.

If you do marry, you have not sinned, but you have entered a life full of many troubles. Remember? Adam's problem was not singleness but being alone, being by himself. And you do not have to marry not to be alone.

Basically, Paul's advice was simple: Do not jump into marriage unless you are sure you have what it takes to make it work, *unless* you are burning with passion. Then you need to find another believer and marry to stay out of sin. However, you still need to make sure you have what it takes to make that union work.

I guarantee that if you marry *just* because of passion, your marriage will be passionately destroyed eventually! Better to take your passion and appetite to the Lord and give it up on the altar. Ask Him to bring you the right mate, if you know that you must marry.

I would write to you, the reader, the same thing Paul did to the Corinthian believers. I am not saying this to put you in bondage, to restrict you, or to tell you what to do. But I am writing in order that you may live in a right way in undivided devotion to God. (v. 35.)

Then Paul explained that widows are free to marry, but *let it be in the Lord*. However, he added, in line with his other advice, ''in my opinion, she is better off to stay single.''

*"When reading the Bible, one
of the most dangerous things
you can do is isolate verses
from their context."*

10

The History of Divorce

In this chapter, we are going to look at the history of divorce among God's people to see why Jesus and Paul had questions to answer and things to straighten out.

Matthew 5:31 begins with Jesus saying:

> **It hath been said, whosoever shall put away his wife, let him give her a writing of divorcement.**

Who said this? The Jewish people whom Jesus was teaching in the Sermon on the Mount knew what Jesus meant. He was referring to the writings of Moses in Deuteronomy.

> **When a man hath taken a wife, and married her, and it come to pass that she find no favour in his eyes** (is not pleasing to him), **because he hath found some uncleanness in her: then let him write her a bill of divorcement, and give it in her hand, and send her out of his house.**
>
> **Deuteronomy 24:1**

When you are reading the Bible, one of the most dangerous things you can do is isolate scripture verses from their *context*. To pull one verse out of a chapter and book and use it as the foundation of some doctrine will cause you to get into error.

The *context* means seeing who the speaker was, who he was talking to, what he was talking about, and why he was addressing that particular subject. We saw a little of that in the last chapter.

We looked at *why* Paul was talking about divorce and saw that he was answering questions concerning specific situations that had arisen within the cultural setting of a certain church.

Jesus: the Wisdom Teacher

Paul wrote in 1 Corinthians 1:30 that Jesus was made of God *wisdom*, righteousness, sanctification, and redemption unto us. Jesus also was a "wisdom teacher."

"Wisdom teaching" was one of the teaching methods of His day. What that means is that the teacher used figures of speech, everyday-life examples, and hyperbole in order to make a point.

We might call it practical, common-sense teaching. *Hyperbole* means to exaggerate something for effect, such as, "He is as strong as an ox."

For instance, when Jesus said, "If your right eye offends you, gouge it out, and throw it away," of course, He did not mean for His hearers to literally gouge out their eyes! It was exaggeration for effect. What He was saying, and what His listeners heard because they were accustomed to this kind of teaching, was:

"If something that you feel is very important and necessary is causing you to sin, get rid of it. It has become more harmful to you than a help."

If a well-paying job is keeping you from fellowship with God, attending church, and spending time with your family, leave it. A less-well-paying job will be of more benefit to you in the long run.

This kind of teaching also used proverbs (wise sayings), riddles, parables (stories of real-life situations with morals), and allegories. Allegories are stories in which one set of things is used in place of another set to make a more graphic picture.

The prophet Nathan went to King David with an allegory. He told the king of a man with one ewe lamb that had been taken away and killed for a feast by a man who already had many lambs. Nathan used "lambs" in place of "wives" to show David how awfully selfish and sinful he had been. (2 Sam. 12:3)

When I first began to read the Bible about divorce, I came away with "dogma" instead of truth. Dogma is:

"I'm right, and you are wrong. It does not matter what you say, and don't confuse me with the facts."

Without studying the Word according to sound principles of interpretation, you are going to come up with a lot of wrong conclusions. You will believe errors because your conclusions are based on insufficient evidence.

Divorce and remarriage is one subject that brings more confusion and puts people under more condemnation than almost any other in the Christian or non-Christian walk.

"Did I sin against God?"

"If God forgave me, why do I still feel guilty?"

"I remarried. Am I committing adultery?"

"Did I do the right thing? Perhaps I should have stuck it out and waited longer to see what would have happened."

If you have been through a divorce, some, if not all, of these questions will have run through your mind.

To see what the Bible really says, we must interpret the verses properly.

Principles of Interpretation

There are three principles necessary for correct interpretation of scriptures:

1. Keep in mind the *literal* thing about which you are reading.

2. Find out the historical setting of the verse or verses. That is the cultural, political, economic, social, and educational environment of the times.

3. Look at the verses that come before the one you are considering and the verses that come after it — the pre-text and the post-text make up the "context" of each verse you read or hear.

No matter whose book you are reading or to whom you are listening, you need to remember that he or she is teaching from a verse that has a *pre-text, a context, and a post-text,* as well as a historical setting. If the teaching is from a verse without taking those things into consideration, the speaker could be teaching error. You could believe something that is not true, if you do not check it out.

So in order to get back to Moses, we must find out what Jesus was literally saying, when He quoted Moses and then expanded on Moses' ruling.

In the Sermon on the Mount, Jesus was giving His hearers the proper attitudes of the Kingdom of God. The context of His comments on divorce was "right thinking" as well as "right actions."

The pre-text of Matthew 5:30,31 is the Beatitudes. People who had those attitudes were the "light of the world."

Then He threw in a caution, a warning to them, not to get off balance on what He was going to say.

In verses 17-20, He said:

"I am going to say some things that may startle you. So, right up front, I want you to remember that I am not coming against Moses, Isaiah, Jeremiah, or any of the other writers of the Law and the Prophets.

"I did not come to do away with what they said. I came to fulfill or complete what they said. Furthermore, if anyone tells you not to obey those writings or ties to do away with them, he will be least in the Kingdom.

"Everything that was said in the Law and Prophets will last as long as heaven and earth lasts. So please don't misunderstand what I am going to say."

Fulfill means "to expose the true intention of." Usually, when people read what Jesus said, they think it means He came to *do* the works of the law. However, that is not what He meant. He came to show them what the law really meant and why it was given.

In essence, Jesus came to give "the spirit of the law"; in legal terms, not what was said, but what was meant.

After His warning remarks, Jesus talked about real righteousness as opposed to outward appearances (religious rituals, and so forth). *Real* righteousness (v.20) means not only do not murder someone, but do not even hate them or wish them dead.

Real righteousness means that you give tithes *and* forgive your enemies. Real righteousness means it is not enough not to actually commit adultery; you must not even lust in your mind or wish you could indulge your passion.

Then He used hyperbole to emphasize all of the things He was saying: **If thy right eye offend thee, pluck it out** (vv. 29,30). After that, He began His remarks about divorce.

The post-text of His divorce comment was the manner in which they took oaths and handled their enemies. In other words, adultery and divorce were in a list of unrighteous things that included everything from hatred to keeping your word to getting even.

The context, as I said above, is that "what you *think* is as important as what you do." Jesus was saying that divorce is not the problem but what leads up to it. Divorce is only the consequence of wrong attitudes toward your spouse. In essence, divorce is the symptomatic manifestation of marital deficiency.

Then in Matthew 19, the context was answering questions of the Pharisees. The pre-text is their questions, and the post-text is the disciples' comments on Jesus' answers.

Now, let us look at Moses' ruling on divorce to see the historical setting of Jesus' remarks.

Where Divorce Began

What is the context of Deuteronomy 24:1? Moses, the lawgiver, collected in one book all of the laws, statutes, civil rulings, and so forth, that God had given him for the nation of Israel. Just as in Jesus' Sermon on the Mount, Moses' remarks are in the middle of a collection of rulings that covered everything from interest rates to health and sanitation to keeping vows.

If you read both sections of Scripture, you will see that Jesus basically was reinterpreting Moses' rulings that covered natural situations. Jesus was *adding* a spiritual dimension to all of Moses' law — not making it less binding, but more. He was putting the "spirit" back into the law.

The attitude of the heart was what counted under the New Covenant He came to establish, not just the actions of the body.

Jesus' focus was not divorce but what *causes* divorce and why Moses insisted on divorce papers in the first place, which was "the hardness of their hearts." (Matt. 19:8.)

What does that mean? Does it mean that because of the hardness of heart, they were committing adultery, so Moses had to let them divorce?

Moses was not even addressing the sin of adultery.

Moses did not mention adultery as a condition for divorce, because there was only *one* consequence of adultery: death by stoning.

So, in Moses' day, there was no divorce on grounds of adultery. However, men were leaving their wives "for any other reason." That is why the Pharisees asked Jesus if it was lawful for a man to put away his wife *for every cause.* (Matt. 19:3.)

Worse still, men could repeat three times "I divorce you" and leave their wives to marry someone else. However, the wives could not remarry without a legal paper, a bill of divorcement. And, many times, they did not have any means of support when their husbands left.

That is the reason for the custom of taking whatever dowry (money given them at marriage by their fathers) and exchanging that for coins to be worn around the neck or hanging from headdresses. Then the wives would have finances if their husbands put them out of the house.

Without understanding the context of Moses' sayings, you cannot understand what he meant. Moses said they could no longer treat their wives that way. If men were going to run off to second wives for *any* reason, they must give their first wives bills of divorcement.

Moses Was Protecting Women

Moses was setting forth a process men had to go through to get rid of their wives: 1) Write her a bill of divorcement, 2) Give it to her, and 3) Send her away.

That phrase "send her away" is a figure of speech used from the time the Israelites were "sent away" by the Egyptians. It meant to send someone off with goods, money, and so forth.

When a master freed a slave, he was to "send them away" with certain things — a certain amount of money, an extra suit of clothes, some cattle. In other words, anyone "sent away" was to have enough to start life over again.

Jesus was saying, "Moses commanded your ancestors to give wives a writ of divorce because their hearts were so hardened they were leaving their wives destitute and without hope for another marriage.

"*But I say* that it is not lawful in the sight of God to leave your wives *for every cause* in the first place. Furthermore, I have come to bring mercy, so instead of stoning a woman caught in adultery, divorce her. And that is the *only* cause for divorce — the breaking of the marriage vows — not every little thing she does that you do not like."

Then Jesus pointed out that what Moses had to allow, God had never intended. God made male and female and joined them. He said for men to leave their parents and *cleave* to (be glued to, chase after, or be united with) their wives. He also said not to let anyone separate the couple bonded together by vows.

Jesus wanted them to think about what *made a marriage* (Gen. 2:24), not the conditions under which they could get out of a marriage. If you have a right marriage, you will not even think about getting a divorce. Your attitude and heart are what counts.

God hates divorce, breaking vows and not keeping your word, but *He still loves divorcees.* Under the New Covenant, any sin but the unpardonable sin (blaspheming the Holy Spirit) is covered by the blood as soon as you repent and receive forgiveness.

Many religious people today act as if divorce is the unpardonable sin, too great a sin for the blood of Jesus to cover. That would make divorce more heinous a crime than murder!

Divorce became more and more prevalent between Moses' day and Jesus' day. Probably, it was almost as common as today. Otherwise, the Samaritan woman who had been married five times and was living unmarried with a sixth man would have been an outcast. Please note the scriptures never said her former husbands were deceased.

Divorce was so common that when God was about to cut the nation of Israel off and then send the nation of Judah into exile, He used marriage and divorce as an allegory to explain the seriousness of what was going to happen to both peoples.

In Jeremiah 3:8, God said He had given "faithless Israel" a Certificate of Divorce and sent her away *because of all her adulteries.* Even that had not caused "faithless Judah," her sister, to turn away from prostituting herself with foreign nations and other gods and return to her true Husband, God said.

Even in Jesus' day, men also practiced polygamy, having more than one wife at a time, although that was not as common as in Abraham's day.

On the other hand, there were some situations where the Lord actually *commanded* the Jews to get a divorce!

Those cases involved the days after the return from Babylonian exile when the Jewish men had married pagan and idolatrous women. (Ezra 10.) The prophet was so grieved that he physically attacked some of the men involved and pulled out handfuls of his own beard. We must not confuse this stand against "mixed marriages" as ethnically based or race-related, but rather as spiritual incompatibility.

He knew mixed marriages with pagans who worshipped idols had led to Israel and Judah's downfall in the first place. He commanded all of the men with "strange wives" to put them away, and the Bible says they all agreed to do so.

The point is that you will get into error by taking one principle or commandment of God and trying to apply it to every situation. Now, I am not talking about "situational ethics" where there is no absolute, and you can bend the rules to suit yourself.

I am talking about finding out from God *which* of His principles or commandments really applies in a situation. Otherwise, you are misapplying the Word, and you can make as big a mistake as deliberate disobedience if you do this.

The principle that governed the situation under Ezra was not Gen. 2:24 about cleaving together and what God had joined. That was not the case at all. God had *not* joined these couples.

The principle involved was **Be ye not unequally yoked together with unbelievers** (2 Cor. 6:14a). The *rest* of that verse says, **For what fellowship hath righteousness with unrighteousness? And what communion hath light with darkness?**

The history of divorce stretches back into antiquity and has been found in every race, nation, and civilization. However, for Israel and later Judah, divorce began with "the Great Lawgiver, Moses."

Everything Jesus, or any other teacher, said had to line up with Moses. And Jesus agreed with that: "If you are getting divorced, give her a bill of divorcement, but the only grounds is adultery."

He not only lined up with Moses, He made the responsibility greater. Intentions and motives became more important under the New Covenant than doing or acting.

In other words, Jesus responded to the question of divorce with an answer about marriage. He was reiterating the principle that, if marriage is properly understood and entered into, there will be no need for consideration of divorce.

*"From the beginning of
the world, God placed the
responsibility of marriage on men."*

11

The Husband's Responsibility

A young man wrote me once and said, "You are hard on us men. You are always coming down on us. Why don't you ease up?"

I replied, "I can't, because I'm one of *us*, and God comes down hard on us."

From the beginning of the earth, God placed the responsibility of marriage on men. The serpent tempted Eve, she picked and ate the fruit, but God headed straight for Adam that evening.

He said, "Adam, where are you, man?"

Adam tried to say, "Lord, that woman *You* gave me," and God said, "Adam, I didn't ask you about the woman. I asked where *you* were."

If you look carefully at Jesus' and Paul's words, you will see they were not really talking about divorce at all. They were talking about marriage.

Just as Jesus told the Pharisees, we must go back to God's original plan for man and woman, in order to see what His intentions were.

In Genesis 2:24, two principles are given for men who marry:

1. *Leave* mother and father.

2. *Cleave* to the woman you marry.

The result? The man and the woman would become *one flesh.*

For this cause is a man to leave his parents. What cause? Because God has provided a mate for you. The cause is two people being in the will of God and in fellowship with God *and* with one another.

Oh, if I could only say that strongly enough! Do not begin a relationship with a woman until you find someone to be with you as Adam and Eve were in the Garden of Eden. The reason you leave your parents, men, is important. If you leave for less than the right God-given relationship, you will probably end up leaving your wife later.

Divorce Means Defecting

The word translated *divorce* in the New Testament is *apostasion,* which has an interesting meaning. The same word is used in the Greek version of the Old Testament which was available in Jesus' day, *The Septuagint.*

That word in Greek means primarily ''a defection''; literally, ''a standing off from.''[1]

You can only *defect* if you have made a commitment to something. A soldier who has enlisted or been drafted for a certain term of service and then runs away without permission is said to be a ''defector.''

The dictionary definition of *defect* is:

1. ''Lack of something necessary for completeness; deficiency; shortcoming;''

2. ''An imperfection or weakness; fault; flaw; blemish;''

Or, in this usage, ''to forsake a party, cause, etc.''

---

[1]Vine, W. E. *Vine's Expository Dictionary of Old and New Testament Words* (Old Tappan: Fleming H. Revell Company, 1981), Vol. I, p. 329.

If you notice, in Genesis, the Word did not say for a *woman* to leave her father and mother and "be glued to" her husband. It said **For this cause should a *man* leave his parents.**

Do you see why Jesus did not even want to discuss divorce? He included the subject in a list of many others to set forth "right thinking" and the spirit of the law. But, otherwise, He only touched on it when asked point blank by religious leaders trying to get Him in trouble.

Divorce is like a soldier going to the general and saying, "I don't like this. I want to be a civilian again."

If a soldier in action defects, he is apt to be shot. Now, do you see why the disciples said it is better not to marry?

According to the Word, if a man takes a wife out of her parent's home, he is to chase after her in hot pursuit (another meaning for the Greek word for *cleave*), and when he catches her, to stick to her like glue.

That means no matter where she goes or what she does, he comes in behind her. His goal is to stick to her. That means they become one, for the most part, based on his efforts.

Basically, what all this means is that God says, "Marriage rests on the shoulders of the husband, and divorce rests on the shoulders of the husband."

Whatever happens in the home is the husband's responsibility. Please note, I did not say it is the husband's *fault*. Also, note that divorce began with men. Because of that, Moses allowed bills of divorcement to protect the women of Israel. Nowhere in the Law did God make provision for divorce.

In all of the commandments, statutes, and civil regulations handed down to Moses by God, there is no provision specifically set out by God giving grounds for divorce. The only thing Moses dealt with was how to protect the helpless wife when her husband walked out on her.

Jesus' disciples understood that He was saying, "When you enter marriage, death is the only way out that God has provided. If the marriage vows are broken, it is permitted to divorce. Even then, the Lord would prefer that you stick it out.

"And, furthermore, you men are responsible for choosing a wife and for seeing to it that the marriage works."

No wonder they decided it was better not to marry!

There are certain things in this world order, which are under satanic control (2 Cor. 4:4), that God did not design. For example, your body is not designed for worry. There is no hormone in the body designed to deal with worry.

That means God in His infinite wisdom never intended for you to worry. That is why people get ulcers. They are under stress and tension and worry, and hormones overproduce to deal with the situation. That burns holes in the lining of the stomach.

In other people, their minds and bodies develop the "holes," and they have nervous breakdowns, need psychiatric help, or actually go insane. Their minds have been trying to deal with something they were not designed for.

As your body was not designed for worry, so your marriage is not designed for divorce. Going through a divorce, no matter how "friendly," leaves you with a sick feeling, a trauma. You go through the same sense of loss, even if you wanted the divorce, that you would if that person died.

People have gotten divorces, been forgiven for breaking vows, and gotten remarried. For the most part, they may be happy. But, somewhere inside, there is still a sick feeling that only the resurrection will totally deal with.

The Social Context

One current event in Jesus' day that brought up this subject was King Herod's taking his brother's wife.

Herod Antipas was one of the sons of Herod the Great, who was king of all Palestine when Jesus was born. He died when Jesus was about six or seven, and the area was divided by Rome into five sections.

Rome directly governed Judea under a governor. (Pontius Pilate was governor when Jesus was crucified.) Galilee, where Jesus was brought up in Nazareth, and Perea were under the rule of Herod Antipas. One of his half-brothers was Herod Philip I, who had married the daughter of still another half-brother, Aristobulus I — in other words, a half-niece.

In the days when John the Baptist was preaching, to pile sin on sin in the eyes of the Jews, Herod Antipas had gotten Herodias, also his half-niece, to leave Philip and live with him.

That caught the attention of John the Baptist, who immediately began to preach vehemently against this union. That incident is what precipitated his arrest and, later, his assassination by Herod Antipas. (Mark 6:17-29.)

Since John told Herod it was not lawful for him to have her (Matt. 14:4), perhaps there was not even a legal divorce, although John may have been referring to the incest involved. Herod, Philip, and Herodias had different mothers, but the same father.

Apparently, the Pharisees were not as concerned about divorce as they were in trying to get Jesus to say something about this situation between Herod Antipas and his brother's wife.

Also, there were two schools of theology (rabbinical teaching) in that day. One held that the word Moses used in Deuteronomy 24:4 was restricted to its exact meaning, **some uncleanness.** The Hebrew is *ervah,* which is only used that one time in the Old Testament and means ''disgrace, blemish,'' or ''shame, unclean.''[2] The other school ruled that ''some uncleanness'' covered a lot of territory; thus, the common use of divorce *for every cause.*

However, Jesus' answer said to them: ''If you cannot live with this person anymore, you can't marry anyone else. You can't even touch anyone else sexually, because you will be causing them to commit adultery along with you. Furthermore, the wife you divorced cannot marry anyone else, and you will be causing her to commit adultery.''

Who Joins a Couple Together?

Matthew 19:6b and Mark 10:9 say:

> **What therefore God hath joined together, let not man put asunder.**

Who joins couples in marriage? Jesus said God does.

God says, ''You chase her, and I will join you. Hang in there, son, I've got the glue!''

Is that not wonderful? We think love (which we usually think of in physical terms) joins a man and woman together, or their home, or their children, or just spending years together.

Not even a legal paper joins them. The marriage license simply makes the joining legal, according to the laws of the land. *Some people may be legally married but not joined.*

If you are married now and having problems, go to God and say, ''Father, we have a problem. We need a Joiner. We need the glue of Your Holy Spirit.''

---

[2]Strong, James. *The New Strong's Exhaustive Concordance of the Bible,* ''Hebrew and Chaldee Dictionary,'' (Nashville: Thomas Nelson Publishers, 1984), p. 91.

God was saying to mankind throughout the Bible, "Your marriages cannot work without Me. I am the glue. I am the Joiner-together."

If God does not join you, man undoubtedly will put you asunder in some fashion down through the years. But if God joins you, no man can put you asunder.

Then Jesus said another shocking thing:

And if a woman shall put away her husband . . . .

Mark 10:12

All during that time, wives could not divorce their husbands. Only husbands could get divorces. Wives were considered property, the same as houses, lands, and animals.

Society had said for hundreds of years that women were not full citizens; therefore, they could not divorce. Then Jesus came along and said, yes, they could, just the same as the husbands.

I encourage you women readers who have been going through such guilt to understand that God is not blaming you. He is looking at the fellow who was to be responsible. I know a lot of men are going to be angry and perhaps write me letters. But God set it up this way — I did not!

You would do better, men, to take a look at your marriage and your family and ask God what you have done and not done. Then repent, and begin to let Him show you how to repair things and mend relationships.

In the Bible, it is always the father whom God admonishes:

Fathers, provoke not your children to wrath. Fathers, lead your children in the paths of God. (Eph. 6:1-4.)

No wonder families are in danger today. This satanic world order has turned things around so that society actually believes it is the mother's role to bring up the children. No wonder kids do not respect authority or are "wimpy." Their fathers were not good role models or caregivers.

You men who are not yet married, please take heed to this revelation. If you are unmarried, be quick to hear and slow to speak. Do not lead women on and play games with their emotions. Make up your mind not to make a move unless you are ready to die for the commitment.

In other words, do not join the army until you are prepared to die and never defect.

Before you start chasing, make sure she is someone you can chase until death do you part. Today, a lot of women are out there advertising, but you men must decide, "Is she chaseable to the grave"?

Check out everything. Most of all, ask God. Seek His will.

And, women, you do the same.

For both sexes, it is important to know that chasing someone who looks nice is apt to be deceiving. What looks nice now may not in ten years, or may not when you see her or him without makeup or with a full beard and unwashed after a hard day's work.

Love someone because of their attitude, character, inner spirit being — all the things that will not change.

It is better to remain unmarried a little while longer than to jump too quickly into what could be a living hell. I have counseled too many people in unhappy marriages over the years not to know that what I am writing is true.

Even different religions can cause a problem. If what you believe is contrary to what the other person believes, you are headed for trouble. You may think now that "love conquers all," but that is just until the honeymoon is over!

Love may conquer a person's physical body, emotions, and mind. But love cannot subdue a person's *will*. That must be surrendered and submitted by the choice of the person.

A submitted body should not be confused with a submitted will or spiritual convictions.

No matter how much you think you love someone, find out *if* they serve God and *how* they serve Him. Make sure that you carry the same firewood to burn on the same altar before the same sacrifice. Otherwise, you have two altars and strange fire, an ungodly situation.

Remember, marriage is more than a legal contract to physically sleep together and share the family financial obligations. Marriage is the joining and uniting of two *souls* wherein lies the center of submission, conviction, values, and moral and spiritual perception. If the souls are not compatible, the relationship is on a course of tragic disaster.

*"If you and I break fellowship,
it hurts God worse than it hurts us."*

12

Broken Relationships

Our study of the Word shows God does not encourage nor make any provisions for separation of something bonded together by Him. He does not condone nor, certainly, enjoy any kind of separation in relationships.

God does not like broken fellowships between different parts of the Body of Christ. He does not like broken fellowships within churches or families. He does not like separations between friends — much less between husbands and wives.

If you and I break fellowship, it hurts God worse than it hurts us. Separation is detrimental to the flow of fellowship.

That is why God said, "If you are out of fellowship with a brother or sister, don't come to Me in prayer or bring offerings until you have mended the broken relationship." (Matt. 5:23,24.)

Broken fellowship in any form is destructive to the person and to his fellowship with God. Broken homes and broken lives are not pleasing to God. They make Him sorrowful.

You can get a broken body mended by modern medicine, unless it is beyond repair. But if you have a broken heart, there is not much a doctor can do. A broken heart actually is a broken soul.

Your soul is your personality: the mind, will, and emotions. If your mind is shattered, your will is broken, and your emotions are wounded, you have no incentive to keep living. You have no desire to keep going forward in life.

The book of Proverbs is a book of wisdom sayings. Some of them really illuminate this area of broken relationships.

> **The beginning of strife is as when one letteth out water: therefore leave off contention, before it be meddled with.**
> **Proverbs 17:14**

> **The spirit of a man will sustain his infirmity; but a wounded spirit who can bear?**
> **Proverbs 18:14**

> **A brother offended is harder to be won than a strong city: and their contentions are like the bars of a castle.**
> **Proverbs 18:19**

In everyday modern English, what those verses are saying it this:

*Beginning a quarrel is like turning on the faucet or making a hole in a dam: what starts as a trickle soon turns into a flood. Forgive and forget.

*A hurt or a wounded spirit is one that is crushed. Not only the soul is involved in broken relationships but the spirit being, the *real* person. You *are* a spirit being who *has* a soul and *lives* in a body.

"Who can bear it?" the author of Proverbs asked. (Prov. 18:14.) The severity of hurt in a broken heart is almost unbearable. I have seen people who have broken up with boyfriends or girlfriends — much less husbands or wives — and have remained messed up emotionally for months.

*If you are the one who is the offender, then you need to understand the consequences of your actions. That last verse quoted is saying:

"If you ever wounded anyone emotionally, psychologically, mentally, or physically, it is almost like breaking into a fortress to get fellowship restored with them."

A "fortified city" had a wall around it that might be up to a half-a-mile wide. There were all kinds of weapons and armor on the wall. An enemy literally could not get near the city.

When the Persians conquered Babylon in the latter days of the prophet Daniel, it was not possible to get through the thick and wide walls of Babylon. The attackers had to divert a stream running into the city and come under the city gates up the stream bed. Attempting to restore a broken relationship could be as difficult as trying to conquer such a fortified city.

Whenever there is a broken or "killed" relationship, you can be sure that God is not involved. Someone else is triggering the destruct mechanism. That one is the thief who comes to kill, steal, and destroy. (John 10:10.)

Experiencing "divorce" means experiencing a broken relationship. That relationship may not be a legal marriage. A legal marriage is the result of an emotional marriage, but not all emotional marriages are legalized.

Emotional Marriage

If you become involved with someone to the extent of seeing them at least three times a week, be careful. You are getting emotionally attached. If you see someone more than six months, you have formed many "soul ties," or emotional bondings. You are becoming dependent on one another emotionally, even if not physically.

When you begin to get emotionally bonded, part of the other person reaches out and sticks to you, and part of you reaches out and sticks to them. That is one kind of "glue" that causes people to *cleave* (stick to) one another.

What happens is almost like throwing cobwebs at one another until you become totally enwebbed in the other person.

Emotional bonding develops slowly, but consistently, and is based on how much time you spend with the other person. Also involved is the amount of communication between you and the other person, the amount of sharing hopes, dreams, inner thoughts.

It can be dangerous, particularly because the process is undetected in most instances. The right kind of emotional bonding obviously is good. A successful marriage will involve two people, who have learned to be single, choosing to become one with each other.

In some families, parents and children are not bonded. Brothers are not bonded to brothers or to sisters. The name for that kind of family relationship is *alienation*. They are related, yet strangers.

Do not confuse being related with bonding. You can be related to someone without strong bonds. Bonding is never a gift, but a result of impact in a relationship.

If there ever comes an occasion for separation of emotional bonding, however, there is no such thing as, "Give me my cobwebs back."

What happens in a separation is that there is an uprooting or a tearing out of both persons. When one rips a part off the other, that part will never be replaced.

Your "web" is all tangled up in the other person's, and theirs is glued with yours. When you are pulled apart, it is like yanking roots out. A wound is left, and wounds bleed.

Emotional marriage also takes place between people who are not legally married. You do not avoid wounds by saying, "Well, let's just quit."

A young lady in my church once said, "Boy, if I were not a Christian, I would *kill* him!"

That was not a right attitude, but I understood how she felt.

To avoid broken relationships, watch your "webs." Protect your "webs." When people begin to get deeper in conversation and start sharing intimate things, the deeper and stronger the webs get.

This may be the most serious part of a relationship. These ties are not broken by going to court and getting a legal divorce. It is possible to be legally divorced but emotionally still married. Lawyer, judges, juries, and courts cannot give you an emotional divorce.

If that relationship is broken at any point, you will experience a "divorce." Your soul is wounded because ties between you and the other person are torn apart.

A betrothal in Bible times was as binding as the wedding itself. They went through a ceremony, and for a period of time, usually a year, the couple got acquainted, found out what each other was like, and prepared their home with its furnishings, linens, and so forth.

It was during this period that the young man (bridegroom) was given a dowry to fulfill the obligation of the bride's father. He had to satisfy the father's requirement before marriage.

The "engagement" involved everything but the physical consummation of the marriage. Until the engagement, the couple was not allowed to spend a lot of time together. After the betrothal, they were considered married, but each still lived at home with his or her parents.

Jesus' mother and stepfather were betrothed, and the relationship was considered so binding that Joseph would have had to legally "divorce" Mary. He considered "putting her away secretly" before the angel of the Lord came to him in a dream and reassured him. (Matt. 1:18-25.)

Joseph had to consider "divorce" because he and Mary were *committed* to one another. The minute you commit yourself to someone else, anything that happens to break up that relationship is an emotional divorce.

But nowhere in God's plan is there a provision for divorce. Nowhere is there an escape hatch. There is no escape clause in marriage where God is concerned. Marriage was not made for divorce.

God created our bodies to heal themselves. If your body gets cut, it can heal itself. God created our minds to hold millions and millions of thoughts and to retrieve those we need. God created your emotions to be able to express feelings and respond and react to things in the environment.

God created the body to receive food, take out nutrients, and to release the waste. But there is nothing in you to handle what God did not make provision for.

God did *not* make provision for you to handle sin. That is why He had to come in and help us. People jump off bridges, jump out of windows, slit their wrists, and drink poison to kill themselves because they cannot handle sin.

So God sent His Son and provided a way to handle sin — the blood of Jesus.

There was nothing created in man to handle the hurt of divorce. Marriage is God's invention; divorce is man's intention. Marriage is not designed for divorce.

Today, a lot of emotional marriages are being broken. Some of them are legal marriages; others are not. Perhaps people have just lived together as man and wife for a number of years. They are emotionally married, and any disruption in that relationship has the same effect as a legal divorce. It is a defection.

Vows and Promises

Separation is the termination of a commitment with emotional involvement. *Divorce* is legalized separation.

If you are separated, but not divorced, I advise you to pray the person you are still married to does not fall into adultery, and neither do you. Then make every effort to work out your differences and get back together.

In that case, repent for making vows you could not keep and for breaking vows. Ask God to forgive and heal your soul over this thing. Then do as Jesus told the woman caught in adultery, "Go and sin no more." (John 8:11.)

A promise is a commitment to do something later, and a vow is a binding commitment to begin doing something now and to continue to do it for the duration of the vow. Some vows, or contracts, are for life; others are for limited periods of time.

A vow is unto death, which is why God said, "Don't make it if you are not going to keep it."

> When thou vowest a vow unto God, defer not to pay it; for he hath no pleasure in fools: pay that which thou hast vowed.
>
> Better is it that thou shouldest not vow, than that thou shouldest vow and not pay.
>
> Ecclesiastes 5:4,5

"Unto death" does not mean "until your natural death." It means giving God the right to allow you to die if you break the vow. Under the Old Covenant, if they broke vows and God's mercy did not intervene, something serious happened.

A vow is not made to another person. Vows are made to God or before God; in other words, with God as a witness.

The Impact of Emotional Defection

Everyone who has been involved in a broken relationship, legally married and divorced or not, goes through the same things. The impact of emotional defection is so serious that the Bible talks about it in terms of almost dying or of literal death.

Nothing in the world hurts like a good friend forsaking you. But why was he or she such a good friend? Because you shared with them on a level so intimate that you needed his or her emotional support to maintain the bonding environment.

When that person breaks away, part of you is gone. I would encourage you to guard and protect your relationships with people. Treat people as you would want to be treated.

Television programs and soap operas make it seem that marriage can be like, ''Well, it's been fun, but I'm tired of you now. I have found another one.''

Television, for the most part, is a world of fantasy. There is no way you can marry someone, stay with them for two years, and then decide you are going to cut it off overnight. Separation and/or divorce will leave you sick for years.

God did not make any escape out of marriage, whether it is legal or not. So separation means you are experiencing something He made no provisions for you to experience. No one can deny the hurt and emotional trauma. Emotional defection produces a broken heart in every case.

But I have good news: There is life after divorce, and we are going to talk about that in the last chapter.

"A trauma is an injury,
a wound, or a shock. It
amounts to an earthquake to
the body, soul, or spirit."

13

The Traumas of Divorce

Two things are involved in divorce: tearing apart emotional bonding, as I discussed in the last chapter, and separation distress.

Everyone has been involved in some kind of relationship that failed — from kindergarten on up through adulthood. In the failing, some of those broken relationships left scars or even sores that have not healed.

A *trauma* is an injury, a wound, or a shock. It amounts to an earthquake to the systems of the body, soul, or spirit. Broken relationships always result in traumas, great or small.

Traumas cause distress, and distress manifests in anxiety. When you begin to be anxious, quite often you become at least somewhat irrational. Being irrational means you begin to act without thinking properly.

If your arm were torn away from your body, there would be tremendous pain; secondly, there would be a loss. Forever after, your nervous system feels as if something is still there. Yet, you are aware that it is gone. Such are the aftereffects of a broken relationship.

Thirdly, there will always be a scar in that place; and, fourthly, you will be handicapped after that. There are things you cannot do as well, no matter how you learn to compensate for what is missing.

Of course, there is always healing. Even after amputation, there is healing, and I will talk about that in the last chapter. There are a great many people still walking around with open wounds.

Immediately after a separation or divorce is not a good time to make major decisions, and certainly this is not a good time to get involved with someone else.

Your wounds are still tender, if not bleeding. There are "cords" hanging from those torn webs of emotional bonding. If you marry a wounded person, they are tender, and if you touch them the wrong way, they yell.

There are people who have been divorced a long time and those cords are still hanging. You cannot close up the holes and empty places by patching over them and trying to bond immediately with someone else. Those new webs will not stick.

Ever hear someone talk about "marrying on the rebound"? That just sets you up for a second trauma of separation.

Distress of Soul

The first thing that happens after a break in the emotional bonding is *distress*. Separation brings distress of soul. The first hurt is intense and sharp, caused by the tearing apart of the bonds.

The distress part includes all of the things you go through after the tearing apart. First, the wound; then, the trauma.

Psalm 18:6 says **In my distress, I called upon the Lord** . . . . Call first upon the Lord when you get caught in a traumatic situation.

When you read or hear of the Coast Guard rescuing someone, they usually say, "We heard a distress signal." Immediately, you picture in your mind someone sitting alone on a desert island or floating out on the ocean in some boat or on some part of a boat, raft, or piece of flotsam.

That is the picture of a distressed person. They feel all alone, in a sinking ship without a lifeboat or life preserver. The psalmist was saying that, in such situations, send your distress signals to God.

Distress involves the same feeling of bereavement that follows a death of someone close to you. The same pattern occurs after loss in a relationship as a loss in death.

You have been accustomed to doing things a certain way to please — or appease — that person, and automatically you keep doing them. You keep cooking certain things certain ways, or arranging the furniture a certain way.

You go to bed at night mourning, or at any rate, feeling a loss. Overnight, somehow, the mind forgets. For a period of time, you wake up feeling okay for a few seconds, then a feeling that something is wrong hits you. Finally, you become aware afresh of the loss, and the wound is opened again.

The music the other person used to like gives you a pang of distress, and so forth.

Even those coming out of unhappy marriages go through this process to a certain degree.

One lady came to me for counseling after divorcing a husband who was an alcoholic. He beat her and treated her pretty badly, until finally, she had enough.

She said, ''I know he didn't treat me right. He used to curse me, beat me, and slap me. But I still miss him.''

I had to explain to her that, bad or good marriage, separation leaves wounds and a feeling of loss whether it is through divorce or death.

Emotional bonding, positive or negative, results in a loss when it is broken.

Another part of separation distress is *depression*, caused by contrasting how you *thought* things were going to be the rest of your life and how they are apparently going to be now.

Following a separation, this feeling hits one or both parties. They begin to think about all the plans and dreams they had together — and now all of those are gone with the wind.

Make sure God is with you during those times, or you could wind up in severe depression. Depression stems from feeling rejected. Even the one seeking the divorce feels rejected. That was part of the reasoning behind the separation.

You feel, ''I have been rejected, and the future I planned cannot come to pass.''

Ephesians 1:6 says something beautiful about rejection: **. . . He hath made us accepted in the beloved.**

That knowledge is your protection.

Many people, even Christians, walk around in depression for years after a relationship has been broken. In previous generations, women who were jilted ''went into a decline'' and sometimes spent the rest of their lives in bed or confined to their homes. Some still opt for this response today.

You need to remember that *separation is just an event, an incident.* It is not the end of your life. Even the death of the other person does not mean *your* death. Loss of someone forever through death or divorce does not mean your life is over.

Three Traumas of Separation

Separation distress results in three basic traumas: *a broken heart, a crushed spirit,* and *a painful soul.*

A broken heart is a terrible experience. Sometimes, your heart literally feels as if it is being ripped apart. Broken hearts are real. They mean broken lives.

But Jesus told His hometown neighbors in Luke 4:18 that He had come **to mend broken hearts,** among other things. A broken heart also means a crushed spirit. Life seems to stop. You want to say, "Stop the world, and let me get off." You do not want to go to work, see anyone, or even eat.

All of those things mean death.

If you do not go to work, your bills will not get paid; if you do not fellowship, you will become isolated and die socially; and, of course, if you do not eat, you will physically die.

A crushed, or broken, spirit is dealt with in Proverbs.

> **A merry heart doeth good like a medicine: but a broken spirit drieth the bones.**
>
> **Proverbs 17:22**

> **A merry heart maketh a cheerful countenance: but by sorrow of the heart the spirit is broken.**
>
> **Proverbs 15:13**

Notice the Word says a broken heart *dries up* the bones. The bones are the factory for blood, and we all know that the life is in the blood. Anything that touches your blood touches your very life and existence.

This verse is saying, "Every time something touches your heart, the core of your life, the very first thing it attacks is the source of your life."

A broken spirit dries up your bones. That means your life is being destroyed. We already have looked at Proverbs 18:14, which says, "Who can bear a crushed spirit?"

Also, we already have talked a little bit about a painful soul and the fact that it results from feelings of rejection and causes depression. Some people even experience emotional suicide.

I know people like this!

People who have committed emotional or mental suicide never have a relationship with anyone again. They never make a try at emotional bonding again; it hurts too much.

Others believe everyone is out to get them. The hurt has resulted in a lack of trust and an expectation of being hurt again.

Those verses in Proverbs, however, show that there is *medicine* for all of these traumas. Jesus is the physician, and the medicine is a cheerful or merry heart, joy and gladness instead of misery.

The antidote for the poison of divorce is found in Psalm 43:5.

> **Why art thou cast down, O my soul? and why art thou disquieted within me? hope in God: for I shall yet praise him, who is the health of my countenance, and my God.**

Regain hope; place that hope in God, not in man. Praise the Lord. Praise and worship do miracles toward restoring a merry, happy heart. Jesus *is* not only God, He is your health.

Psalm 34:17-19 says that when the righteous cry, no matter how many their afflictions, the Lord *will* deliver them out of their troubles.

When I read that verse, I said, "God, does that mean when someone is going through a divorce, You are nearer to them than You ever were?" The Lord answered, "Yes."

That is the time you feel He is fartherest away, yet that is when He is nearest. God said He was near to the brokenhearted and will save those (make whole again) with a crushed spirit.

The important thing to learn from all this, if you have been through such a separation or divorce and can identify with these feelings, is that this is a normal pattern. You are not unique in this experience.

But you can see also that there is help in God. You do not have to let all of these feelings and problems control your life. Begin to take control of them and turn them over to Jesus. He is the Healer, and He will heal you, if you let Him.

The Trauma of Church Reaction

I realize that many churches have difficulty with divorce, or with divorce and remarriage. Then there are those who believe that a divorce means you have failed, that you are a second-class citizen.

There are churches where, if you get a divorce, the church rejects you, and your friends leave you. If you are a minister, you can never get in the pulpit again.

Those people are misinterpreting what Jesus said.

He said, "Divorce is real, but it is not God's perfect design for man."

Also, those churches that never teach on divorce because they do not know what to say are not meeting the needs of their congregations. Three out of four marriages end in divorce today in most western societies, which means that most congregations have hurting people sitting there.

It is very hurtful to go through a trauma like divorce and have the people who claim to have the love of God give you a cold shoulder. That is not walking in the love of Jesus.

That is high-minded religiosity; and, really, it is modern Pharisaism to adhere rigidly to the letter of the law and totally miss the spirit of the Word.

There is only one unpardonable sin — and divorce is not it. Divorce — and even divorce and remarriage if they are considered sin — are not sins too big for the blood of Jesus. Yes, divorce is wrong, but so is unforgiveness and judging.

Divorce does *not* mean eternal damnation! Neither does remarriage.

Those who have never experienced the trauma that results from a broken relationship of the magnitude of a divorce should be thankful and grateful to God. Also, however, you should not pass judgment and place condemnation on those who have. Yes, God hates divorce, and divorce is defection or "backsliding" on a commitment. But God loves the divorcee and declares that He is "married to the backslider."

*"Never confuse who you are
with what you have done."*

14

The Aftermath of Trauma

There are things a judge does not tell you when you get a divorce. The courts are not equipped to help you deal with the aftermath. How you handle things is not their business.

And, as I said in the last chapter, many churches — whose business is helping hurting people — ignore the problem. Or perhaps, worse, they add rejection to the rejection divorced people already have.

Above all, do not think you are a failure because a relationship failed. *Never confuse who you are with what you have done.* Smart people may do some dumb things. "Smart" does not mean perfect.

And, *do not confuse failing with failure.* You may have failed, but you are not a failure. Do not measure your self-value by whether or not you make mistakes. *Measure your personal worth by the fact that God gave you value before anyone ever met you.* He loved you enough to send His Son to redeem you *if there had been no one else on earth!*

Say, "That relationship failed, but I am not a failure." Then begin to pick up the pieces, all of the debris and broken parts, give them to God, and ask Him how to go on from there.

The Pharisees judged the woman taken in adultery a failure because of her actions. Jesus judged the actions and told her to go on and not do those things anymore. He forgave her actions and gave her back self-worth.

Typical Ways of Reacting

After a traumatic experience such as a divorce, separation, or being jilted, different individuals react and respond to these events in different ways. Let us take a look at some of these reactions.

The first way people usually react in times of great loss is to *withdraw,* a result of rejection, depression, and great hurt. This basically is pride.

The second way is to become *"a social butterfly."* This is "getting even" and arises out of anger.

The third reaction is to feel the ground sink under your feet and react by trying to *jump to another nearby "rock."* Many times, this stems from fear or panic.

This person operates with "mixed feelings," and stays in a state of confusion. This means wavering back and forth between ways of acting, thinking, and believing. Essentially, this is *double-mindedness.*

When you get a divorce, some of the ground on which you have been standing is shaken or completely torn away.

The only person who handles loss without any unmanageable shaking or ill effects is someone whose foundation is Jesus, someone who solidly stands on the Rock that will never be moved.

The fourth reaction is *to become truly independent.* This person has achieved balance and is on the way to being healed.

Withdrawal Into Self

Most of the time, the immediate reaction of those hurt by separation, divorce, or death is to become introverted.

However, by withdrawing into yourself, you are isolated from help. You have imprisoned yourself within yourself.

Proverbs 28:26 holds wisdom for this type of wrong reaction. It is wrong because it is counter-productive to healing. But it is the "natural" or "normal" thing to do.

> **He that trusteth in his own heart is a fool: but whoso walketh wisely, he shall be delivered.**

How do you "walk wisely"? You walk with the Holy Spirit. You seek the Lord to walk with you. In times of great trauma, it is particularly dangerous to "trust in your heart." A wounded heart is in a weak and dangerous state and vulnerable to irrational behavior.

I do not want anyone who has done any of these things to feel condemned. The Lord does not bring us condemnation (Rom. 8:1), but conviction. I want to bring these insights as illumination, as revelation from God that will dispel the darkness through which you may be walking.

God's way always is opposite to the "normal" way of doing things in the natural world. In the world, you hoard and keep money in order to get more; in God's Kingdom, you give money away in order to get!

Isolation causes you to do all sorts of things: stay home alone, go out to eat and sit by yourself, choose the back row away from everyone at church, not talk to anyone about your situation.

The Bible says you are foolish to try to work things out alone. God did not design mankind to be alone, remember? He did design them to be single, totally the person he made them, whether you are married, unmarried, widowed, or divorced, but not alone.

God said to Adam, "It's not good for man to be alone." (Gen. 2:18.)

A person walking in isolation is trying to use hurt pride to bandage a pained soul, and it may cover the wound from you, but it never keeps it from hurting. Isolation will not bring healing to that sore.

A person walking alone is also suffering from self-pity. First they put on bandages of pride, then comfort themselves with self-patting.

They walk around saying, "I don't need anybody! Besides, I am obviously not worthy of anyone. I'm a failure. I am not worth anything to anyone else."

This is self-deception and must be cancelled.

Replacing Pain With People

If you take the second common way of dealing with trauma, or if you walk through the first stage and move into the second, you attempt to replace pain with people.

That is a dangerous thing to do. This is the stage where you could fall into another relationship that would fail just as the other. This is where "remarriage or a relationship on the rebound" occurs. (The third stage also holds this same danger.)

At this point, a person who has suffered a divorce or a separation wants to say, "Who needs you? I'll show you I don't need you!"

Then they become a "social butterfly," going to the other extreme from isolation. They may bounce from one relationship to another — go out with anyone, perhaps sleep with anyone just to prove a point, go to every club, every church, every gathering.

Instant relationships are no guarantee of *instant relief* from pain. They only camouflage the wound, and it still receives no healing.

Perhaps, instead of seeking gaiety, the person choosing this way of dealing with the trauma finds a group of others with similar hurts. But hurt people cannot help hurt people.

That is the old adage about the blind leading the blind and both falling into the ditch.

They come to me!

In essence, if you want to be successful, do not keep company with failures.

It is okay to try to help friends whose experiences you can identify with, but not until you are at least on the way to healing. You can tell where you are by whether or not you can talk freely about your experience without pain or any negative emotions.

Yes!

And do not let others in the same boat be the only people with whom you associate.

Some people combine these two ways of reacting. They are isolated inside, but deny it by staying in crowds or around other people.

These are the Christians who hide their feelings in church or among friends and smile brightly, while dying inside.

They will say, "Praise the Lord, everything is okay. Jesus is handling all of this. I am fine."

Jesus *can* and *will* handle it; however, in these cases, they are not allowing Him to handle it. They are *denying* there is any problem. Jesus will not work anything on earth without involving His Body.

Looking for A Security Blanket

Amen!

People who have not become truly single, who do not know who they are in Christ, who do not have a firm identity of their own, will react to separation by reaching quickly for another person or group to hold them up.

This reaction also can result in moving too quickly into another relationship. Whatever the reasons for separation and divorce, there needs to be time to back off and see what *your* contribution was to the failed relationship.

If *you* have not been changed for the better in some way from the experience, what is to prevent the next relationship from going the same way — or worse?

Also, you may try to hang onto some vestige of the relationship. You may try to keep the one who left as a friend, or to maintain contact on some other basis.

Former husbands drop in to see if their wives need this fixed or that, or to see if she is okay. Former wives need things fixed, or they need to talk about the children, and so forth.

Some people go back home to Mama and Daddy. They are not stable in themselves, and they made the other person — or the relationship itself — their foundation. Now they seek desperately for stabilization.

Others throw themselves into a job or career and become workaholics. Work becomes their husband or wife, their security blanket. Work becomes a "solid foundation," something on which they can count and through which they can fill their days.

But what happens if the job fails? What happens when retirement comes? The trauma from the failed relationship will be exposed. Even if they managed to remain standing after the first "earthquake," this failure may knock them off their feet for sure.

Sooner or later, wounds have to be healed — not ignored or covered with various kinds of "bandaids" — or eventually death will result. Infections occur, maggots (demonic pests) work into the festering wounds, handicapped areas increase, and all of these lead toward death of some kind.

The "maintenance contact" I mentioned above is common at this stage of reaction. People feel they cannot get along or cannot live together, but they have too many "cobwebs" entangled with the other.

So they set up situations where there has to be contact with the other sometime. One of the two drags out the legal end of it just to stay in touch.

One will say, "I'll come and see the children," or "I'll come and put gas in your car."

This happens with relationships between friends as well, whether there actually has been an affair or just a boy-girl friendship. They break up, but one or both will come to church because they know the other will be there.

One will sit on one side, the other somewhere else. But they see each other and say "Hi." They are aware of one another, or at least, one of them is. That one is maintaining contact.

People legally divorced will still check on one another. Who is he dating? Who is she seeing? Is that person prettier or richer or smarter than me?

People have been apart for months, and yet emotionally, the cords are still there. They need to maintain contact. Some people become good friends after a divorce.

Suddenly, the other person does not look so bad. I know divorced people who could not stand each other while they were married. Yet, now they have lunch together, they go for drives together, they go to parties at friends' houses.

This is "mixed feelings," or "having your cake and eating it too."

All of these behaviors are attempts to weave a security blanket to cushion and comfort you from the emotional trauma. Be sure your security is in Christ and the Word for only they will not pass away.

Regaining Custody of Yourself

To be healed from trauma, you must regain custody of yourself. People think about custody of the children, custody of property, even custody of pets. But few think about regaining custody of themselves. That self which had been placed, at least to some extent, in the keeping of another must be re-accepted or taken back.

This means finding a balance, setting priorities, and dealing with emotions — not repressing them, but dealing with them.

First, the situation must be accepted, not denied, no matter how it hurts. Secondly, you need to get counsel before making any decisions. That means from the Word, from the Holy Spirit in prayer, and from people you can trust.

This reaction will be doubly hard if you were not single, or independent, before you married. If you married in dependence, this will really be difficult.

After a certain time of being glued to someone else, divorce means you have been given a declaration of independence against your will.

A woman now has to face paying her own bills, taking care of children by herself, planning for the future alone.

A man must face eating out all the time or doing his own cooking, not seeing his children day to day as they grow up, and washing his own clothes.

Both must deal with awakened sex drives.

There is a possible danger in regaining custody of yourself, however. That is going to the extreme, violating the very foundational principle of God with mankind: people need people.

Custody of oneself does not mean declaring independence from the human race or establishing a policy of isolation in your own little world. It does not mean to become so self-centered that you declare love bankruptcy and close your *trust* company.

Regaining custody of yourself means that you take responsibility for restoring your life according to God's principles and submit to His healing process. It means to take your roots out of other people and yet develop the freedom to share your fruit with them.

*"People who have been hurt
can be dangerous."*

15

Emotional Aftershocks

Certain emotional aftershocks accompany trauma, like waves that run through the nervous system following physical traumas.

Many times, the first one is numbness, the emotions go into shock and are temporarily paralyzed. This enables some people to continue functioning for a period of time. But when it wears off, look out! The pain suddenly will be almost unbearable.

These emotions also are like smaller shocks that follow a major earthquake. Sometimes, they do almost as much damage. They include anger, the self-pity we already have talked about, panic or fear, irritability, and mood swings.

People who have been hurt can be dangerous. Have you ever seen a dog who was in great pain, yet you could not get close enough to help it? The animal would snarl, and perhaps even bite, if you reached out a hand.

First Corinthians 13:5 says that real love is not easily provoked. What that implies is that things in life have the potential to make you very angry. There is an anger that is righteous, and that emotion will allow you to make right decisions and do right things.

Ungodly anger, however, will cause you to do all the wrong things, to lash out and hurt others because you have been hurt, like a dog in pain.

Several things to remember about anger are these: Do not sin (Eph. 4:26,27) by retaliating or striking out at someone else. Do not curse anyone, nor throw anything you do not want thrown back! Do not do anything foolish.

Anger is a temporary attitude which can cause behavior with permanent effects. Many separations are the result of someone's temporary fit of anger and of things said in anger.

We have already talked about self-pity, and it is a seductive emotion. You can become addicted to feeling sorry for yourself and ruin your whole life.

Panic is a serious thing. When panic strikes, reason vanishes. This is the emotion that leads you to do irrational things.

Panic causes you to sell yourself short. People have married in a state of panic: "I'm not getting any younger. This may be my last chance." Another old adage says, "Marry in haste; repent at leisure." That means you probably will be a long time regretting your haste.

Deal with panic by asking yourself, "Are things really as bad as they seem?" Begin to take stock of your assets and of the possible advantages of your changed situation.

Panic is *fear* in action. Panic always begins with a fear of some kind.

Fear usually stems from insecurity, from not having a firm foundation of love and trust. Fear is never of God.

> **For God hath not given us the spirit of fear; but of power, and of love, and of a sound mind.**
>
> **2 Timothy 1:7**

A sound mind means *correct thinking*. Stop the minute fear strikes, and think. I promise you that if you can stay rational long enough, you will see that whatever you were afraid of is not that bad.

The shadow of death never killed anyone, yet David wrote that he would not *fear* the shadow of death. (Ps. 23:4.) Most of our fears turn out to be ''shadows'' and not the real thing.

Insecurity breeds fear. Because you were hurt, you become afraid to trust anyone else. You may not want to get too close to other people again.

''To be irritable'' or ''irritability'' comes from the word *irate.* An irritable person is one on the verge of anger, one just waiting for a trigger to be pulled, or a button pushed, to explode. Irritability is the pre-anger stage.

Mood swings are when one minute you think, ''I can't stand it without him. I really miss that idiot.'' But the next minute, you think, ''Who needs him? I'm better off without him.''

This state may lead into the ''mixed feelings'' stage or the ''maintenance contact,'' where the person is willing to settle for limited contact rather than total separation.

However, mood swings usually are between highs and lows, while ''mixed feelings'' waver between love and hate. The ''highs'' are happiness and joy, while the ''lows'' are defeat and depression.

Any of these emotional aftershocks may lead to something called ''mental or nervous breakdowns.''

''Breakdowns'' Are Escapism

This is when your ability to handle stress is tested. Stress taken to the extreme will produce breakdown. Nerves do not break down, actually. What ''breaks down'' is the person's mental capacity to deal with things.

People were not able to work things through mentally, so they ''escaped'' into some sort of unreality, some sort of fantasy. They either began to deny what had happened or to make up something else.

They take refuge in unreality. If you cannot deal with what is really going on, you tend to create a world where you can.

Do you remember when you were in school and an exam was scheduled for which you were not prepared?

You might pray for the sun not to come up, for the night to be longer, as I did. Or you might fantasize that you were sick in order to stay home. In many instances, people literally become ill.

That is ("temporary insanity.")

There are people living in various stages of emotional aftershocks and breakdowns following separations and divorces. Many of them are good looking, well-dressed, and smiling, but they are not dealing with reality. They are living in some kind of fantasy.

The progression is this: Numbness, reactions based on emotional shockwaves, then recovery *or* chronic emotional sickness.

Survival Mechanisms

I have discussed the traumas involved in loss through separation, death, or divorce. I have talked about various reactions to loss. I have talked about emotional aftershocks that follow such upheavals. Now, I want to talk about various techniques for handling these situations.

What all these things boil down to is that there are four basic ways to survive. There are four choices of how to handle loss of a relationship:

1. Did you avoid facing the situation, either mentally, emotionally, or literally?

This means that you got caught up in all of the emotion and chose maintenance contact, getting lost in a group, or moving into isolation.

If you are avoiding facing the loss, that means you refuse to talk about it; you avoid people who want to ask you questions; you avoid situations that remind you of the past.

2. Did you escape the situation in some way? Did you move into a fantasy world or into a quick new relationship?

People try to escape one hurt by replacing the relationship with another, and we have talked already about how dangerous that is.

3. Did you deny what happened? This last one is most serious, because it leads to mental or nervous breakdown.

Denial is a serious problem among a lot of "Word people," Spirit-filled, positive-confession Christians. They feel that to admit they are hurting is admitting a failure of faith.

They hide in the cloak of false spirituality. Hurting people attend a lot of prayer meetings. They pray loudly for other people, but will not admit they need prayer. That seems to them to contradict positive confession.

They need to say, "Help! Can anyone pray for me? I'm hurting. This thing is killing me."

Instead, they deny reality. They say, "I'm not hurting. I took it to the Lord and left it there," yet at 2 a.m., they are tossing and turning with a load of distress. Real faith is more than mental assent.

4. Did you face facts, accept reality, and move into the openness required to deal with consequences, effects, and results?

I am sure many readers are wondering, "How do you move into openness? It is easy for you to talk about being open. But it is harder to do. How do I do it?"

There is a "door" that will take you into the openness you need to allow God to heal you. And only God can heal a broken heart.

The Way Out

There is a way out, a stage of recovery that is healthy. That is *openness*.

Openness is an honest desire to face the truth and deal with change. Openness allows you to begin making plans about the future, not spend hours reliving the past.

Acceptance of what has happened and learning how to go on requires openness. What may help is the understanding that everyone goes through this experience to one degree or another in various ways.

A little boy whose pet dog is run over has to deal with all of these things, just as an adult does after a loss. Life is a process of change. Only God remains the same. Society changes, nations change, people change.

The Apostle Paul understood this when he wrote:

> . . . **But this one thing I do, forgetting those things which are behind, and reaching forth unto those things which are before.**
>
> **Philippians 3:13**

He was talking about things in his ministry and looking forward to finishing his earthly race with honor. But the same principle applies in moving on from the past to the future in any area.

You cannot live a healthy life and live in the past. Do not let the failures of the past interfere with your future.

You must let the past be past and move on to the next arena.

There is life after divorce, life after separation, life after a loved one dies, and life after being jilted. But you first have to find your hope in God.

Paul continued in Philippians to say, **I press toward the mark for the prize of the high calling of God in Christ Jesus** (v. 14).

Notice, he did not say, "I press on toward the next town, or the next revival, or the next journey." Those things were the result of his pressing on toward Jesus and His purpose for his life.

You cannot move into openness and healing through another marriage, another boyfriend, another relationship. *You must set your eyes on Jesus and His purpose for your life.*

If you are divorced or have been through the breaking up of a relationship in any way, look at the things I have covered in this chapter. If you will admit where you are, this book can help you through the trauma and to get your life back on track.

"Forgiveness removes any walls between you and God. Forgiveness is vertical as well as horizontal."

16

Life After Divorce and Separation

The key to openness, the door to healing and life after divorce, is *forgiveness*. You need to understand clearly, however, that forgiveness does not get rid of the hurt. What it does is open you up to the One who *can* get rid of the hurt.

No psychiatrist, no psychologist, no counselor can heal a broken heart. Jesus was anointed to heal the brokenhearted. But you have to make your heart available to Him.

Forgiveness removes any walls between you and God. Forgiveness is vertical as well as horizontal. Let us say it the other way around: Unforgiveness toward a human being also blocks your fellowship with God.

In the beginning, I had a problem with defining forgiveness. I thought forgiveness was when you walked up to someone and said, "Well, you hurt me, you know, but you are lucky. Jesus has saved me. I'm only forgiving you because I am a Christian. I want to knock you down, but Jesus won't let me." That is not true forgiveness.

Sometimes hurt even turns into hate, and then the devil is in the driver's seat. When you find out your spouse has been unfaithful, you may want to kill him or her.

God says, "The hurt is inevitable; the anger is okay if it is against ungodliness; but, the hatred is not of Me."

Anger that has turned to hatred means you have judged someone else and are blaming them. When you begin to see them as the source of your problems, unforgiveness has gained hold on your heart.

> **For if ye forgive men their trespasses** (when they sin against you), **your heavenly Father will also forgive you:**
>
> **But if ye forgive not men their trespasses** (their sins against you), **neither will your heavenly Father forgive your trespasses.**
>
> **Matthew 6:14,15**

Mark 11:25 says almost the same thing. When you pray, if you have anything against anyone else, forgive them so that the Father may forgive you.

If you are not the sinned-against but the one who sinned, then I want you to think about this: Asking forgiveness is never honest if you justify your behavior. You are saying, in that case, circumstances warranted what you did. That means that if the same situation arises again, you probably would do the same thing again. That kind of attitude expresses no real sorrow and no repentance.

Forgive in the Hebrew means "to cut loose." In other words, when you forgive someone, you release that person from everything for which you were holding them accountable. When you ask forgiveness, you are admitting accountability. You are expressing sorrow for your behavior and asking that you be released from what the other person holds you accountable for.

If you have a wrong attitude, it gets in God's way. It blocks the flow of His Spirit to you. It means God must withhold from you many blessings that otherwise might come your way. Unforgiveness binds you to that other person with ungodly ties. To be free, you must release them. That releases you into openness.

Remember that forgiveness will not relieve the hurt. But when you are free, God can easily wash the bitterness, anger, and hatred away. Also, you do not have to *feel* like forgiving. Forgiveness is not an emotion but a decision, an act of your will. *Choose* to obey the Word and release the other person. The good feelings will come later.

Forgiving the other person will allow you to accept the reality of the situation. It will bring you to the point where you can tell the Lord you are hurting and scared.

Isaiah 43:2 talks about God's presence with His people:

> **When thou passest through the waters, I will be with thee; and through the rivers, they shall not overflow thee: when thou walkest through the fire, thou shalt not be burned; neither shall the flame kindle upon thee.**

Would most of you who have been through separation, divorce, or otherwise loss of a relationship agree that it was like passing through the waters? How about fire and flood? It seems as if everything is falling apart, and you are drowning in life.

But the Bible says that *if you put your trust in God,* He will bring you through. He did not say you would not ever walk through the fire and flood. God said the storms of life would not overflow you nor burn you up.

To walk in forgiveness and peace in God requires maturity. An immature Christian may *gain* maturity through traumatic experiences, however, if he or she will follow what the Word says.

The Maturing Process

In the book of Luke, there is a verse about how Jesus grew up. It says:

> **And Jesus increased in wisdom and stature, and in favour with God and man.**
>
> **Luke 2:52**

There are four things in that verse that Jesus did, and you must increase in those same four things in order to be spiritually mature.

1. He was a physical being, and so are you. He grew physically.

2. He increased in wisdom. That means Jesus' ability to deal with the issues of life increased. Wisdom begins in the spirit being and through the Word, but it is expressed through the mind.

3. He increased in favor with God. Jesus made sure that His relationship with the Father always was right.

4. He also found favor with His fellow man. He got along peaceably with those in His family and those around Him.

These four things make up what I call "a balanced life." Maturity consists of a balance between all of these things. Following a divorce or separation, these four things must be restored to balance for you to get on with your life.

Wisdom: When you have been hurt, do not allow your mind to turn off. Proverbs 16:9 says to make your plans and God will work out your steps. Do not sit and die. Come up with another plan.

To come up with a plan, you have to think. Impulsively jumping into another relationship, or wallowing around in all of those emotional shockwaves, or escaping into unreality are not rational reactions. They are simply reacting like a mindless being.

If your husband wants to leave, let him take his clothes, his money, even his car (or hers, if it is a wife) but do not let the one who walks out take *your* sanity. You keep your mind intact. You need it for wisdom.

You also need to keep growing. Jesus increased in "stature," and that can mean spiritually, as well as physically.

Stature: However, many people stop taking care of the body in the aftermath of a divorce or separation loss. Because they lose interest in food and do not eat properly, they lose energy.

Loss of energy affects the nervous system, so irritablility results. That sometimes triggers the other emotional aftershocks. *Make yourself eat,* and eat right. Eat for energy.

If your body is fit, you can handle emotional things. If your body is weak, fat, and sloppy, without the stuff to run it, an emotional trauma can kill you. When trouble comes and your heart beats faster, you could have a heart attack. Some people physically die from a "broken heart."

Favor With God: Times of trouble certainly are the times to find favor with God, of all times! Proverbs 3:5 says to trust God with all your heart. That chapter also reminds us not to trust our own understanding.

> In all thy ways acknowledge him, and he shall direct your paths.
>
> Be not wise in thine own eyes: fear the Lord, and depart from evil.
>
> It shall be health to thy navel, and marrow to thy bones.
>
> **Proverbs 3:6-8**

Favor With People: Jesus liked people. He mingled with all types of people from all walks of life. He did not isolate Himself. The only time He went aside was to have private talks with the Father.

When you are hurting, check your social thermometer. However, be selective about those with whom you spend time. Jesus did not spend a lot of time with the religious leaders of His day, who operated in hypocrisy and legalism.

Make sure the people you are around are open and accepting people themselves, able to reach out in love. The Golden Rule will help you here. Give out to others in trouble what you need.

Focus on God

I cannot stress too much the importance of *focus on God*. Do not look at the circumstances, look at the Answer. Make sure Jesus is your foundation, and you *can* have a life after divorce.

Do not focus on yourself and how you feel. Self-focus keeps you from the very healing you need. Self-focus is self-destructive.

Do not focus on the problems of living alone again. This can cause you to do the opposite of the Golden Rule: to *use* people to meet your needs without caring about theirs.

If you reach out frantically to others for the wrong motives, you will exploit them. You will use them sexually, financially, emotionally and not care about them at all. That will cause you to possibly put them through what you have just been through.

Do not focus on what other people think.

Do not focus on a new relationship. Reality is building your world again, not looking for a new one. Focusing on finding another person for a new relationship usually is operating on the falsehood that, "Since that person was not the *right one*, I must go find the right one."

The Bible says God will keep you in perfect peace, if your mind is stayed on Him. (Isa. 26:3.) John 10:10 says that Jesus came for you to have abundant life.

Take your burden and your hurts to God. Call on Him in your distress. After all, even marriage is temporal — for the duration of this life — but your relationship with God is eternal.

The Healing Process

As with everything else, God's Kingdom has an opposite that the devil has developed in this world.

Isolating yourself from people, pulling your hurts around in a garment of self-pity and self-protection, is the opposite of something I call *solitary healing*.

There *is* a time period when you need to be alone. You do not need to be alone with yourself or alone with your hurts. You need to be alone with God.

There is a difference. Do not put on the "golden oldies" of your love life when it was young and thrilling. Do not get alone with old photograph albums. Instead, sing praise songs to the real love of your life: Jesus. Praise and worship put balm on the wound; the other rubs salt in the hurts.

When you are the sickest physically, the hospital generally puts you in intensive care, a solitary place. In times of intense emotional or spiritual sickness, the "intensive care unit" is your solitary prayer closet. (Matt. 6:6.)

When people begin to talk about you, withdraw to a place alone and pray. In a hospital, there comes a time for the "no visitors" sign to go up. In your healing process, there is a time for "no visitors" as well. However, God should not be considered a visitor. He *lives* within you. He is a part of you. Get alone with Him.

This openness to Jesus will keep you from becoming too independent, a real danger after trauma. Your security is not yourself, and it is not other people. Nor is security your job or the government. Your security is Jesus.

The second phase of healing is the opposite of losing yourself and your problems in other people. I call this *community healing*.

The Church of Jesus Christ is a "community of believers." It is supposed to be like a hospital with different local bodies having different areas of specialties in healing, and other medical needs.

Hebrews 10:25 says not to forsake assembling together. Those people about whom this was written were those who had isolated themselves from the Body. We hear the same thing today. People will say they do not need to go to church to worship God, which is true. But they need to go to church to *obey* God and to have people to stand with them. There is strength in numbers.

First Corinthians 12:14 is another place where Paul stressed that every part of the Body *needs* the others. No one part can stand alone. In Galatians 6:2, Paul wrote that Christians are to bear each other's burdens.

There are people out there who can help you. Later, you can help others. It is wonderful to go to the hospital and tell someone, ''I was sick with that same illness, and I came through.''

You need to go to your ''family.'' In the entire New Testament, the word *family* is only used once, in contrast to the many times it was used in the Old Testament. And it is significant that in the one reference, *family* does not mean earthly relatives but the Body of Christ.

> **For this cause I bow my knees unto the Father of our Lord Jesus Christ,**
>
> **Of whom *the whole family* in heaven and earth is named.**
>
> **Ephesians 3:14,15**

Your hurt is not unique. You are not the only one who has ever experienced all of this. Instead of asking, ''Why me?'' as if you were so unique that none of life's problems could touch you, say:

''Why not me? I'm not immune from the storms of life, nor the attacks of the enemy. But I do not have to allow this to defeat me and ruin the rest of my life.''

Trying to handle it yourself in any of the ways we have talked about, however, will result in defeat. There is only one way to gain victory, and that is by going to Jesus and *really* letting Him have the problem.

As I've just said, you cannot release yourself or release the problem and the hurts to Jesus, if you have not released the other person through forgiveness.

When Jesus healed someone, He sent them back to their homes to witness of Him to friends and relatives. I believe the same thing applies here.

The real principle is counterfeited by "maintenance contact," by the mixed feelings of not totally letting go of something that is over. You need to forgive anyone in your family or in the other person's family — or in your church — who contributed in any way to what happened.

Then you need to ask them to forgive you. What you thought was absolutely right and righteous, they may have seen as something else. In your trauma, you may have offended someone.

Divorce affects the extended family, not just the two persons involved. You must remember that, as a citizen of the Kingdom of God, your first responsibility is to love without discrimination.

You may not choose who is worthy of your love. You must love even those who despitefully use you, according to Matthew 5:44. That verse says to *pray* for those people, but you cannot pray genuinely for someone without beginning to love them.

In your own self, of course, this is like everything else. *Without God, you can do nothing* (John 5:30, 15:5), but with Him, nothing is impossible. (Luke 1:37.) When you love the Lord with your *whole* heart, then His love flows through you to others. (Matt. 22:37.)

Summary of Healing

The door to healing is *openness*, and the key is *forgiveness*. The first step is *solitary healing* — just you and

God. The second step is *community healing* — fellowship with the rest of the Body.

Keep your focus on God, and you can say, ''Father, this is a bad experience. This relationship has failed, but I am a beautiful person because You love me and are making me beautiful.''

The end result will be maturity, gaining in wisdom and stature, and favor with God and man. This balance will cause you to be truly single, if you have not been before.

There *is* life after divorce. Death of your future and defeat does not have to be the result of divorce or separation. The choice is *yours* to make. No one can make it for you.

Life after divorce for you may mean living in your kingdom relationship: just you and Jesus. We already have seen that God hates divorce, but it is not the unpardonable sin. You can be forgiven, even if you were the guilty party, the one who caused it or the one who left the other.

Once you are forgiven, however, *go and sin no more.* Walk through all of the steps to maturity in order not to make the same mistake again.

On the other hand, there may be another marriage for you. But first, become truly single this time, so that you can hear the Lord about His will for you. Marriage should never be for any other motive, by either party, than for God's will. Then there will not ever be a divorce or separation.

If you are unmarried now for whatever reason, go back and read the beginning of this book all over again. All of the insights God gave me about choosing to be married or unmarried and about choosing a mate will help you now.

I trust the Holy Spirit, Giver of all revelation, that this book has blessed your life and will continue to do so.